CAMBRIDGE PRIMARY
Mathematics

Games Book

Emma Low

CAMBRIDGE
UNIVERSITY PRESS

University Printing House, Cambridge CB2 8BS, United Kingdom

One Liberty Plaza, 20th Floor, New York, NY 10006, USA

477 Williamstown Road, Port Melbourne, VIC 3207, Australia

314–321, 3rd Floor, Plot 3, Splendor Forum, Jasola District Centre, New Delhi – 110025, India

79 Anson Road, #06–04/06, Singapore 079906

Cambridge University Press is part of the University of Cambridge.

It furthers the University's mission by disseminating knowledge in the pursuit of education, learning and research at the highest international levels of excellence.

www.cambridge.org
Information on this title: www.cambridge.org/9781107614741

First published 2014
20 19 18 17 16 15 14 13 12 11 10

Printed in Dubai by Oriental Press

A catalogue record for this publication is available from the British Library

ISBN 978-1-107-61474-1 Paperback

Cover artwork: Bill Bolton

CD-ROM Terms and conditions of use

Contents

Introduction

This Games Book consolidates and reinforces mathematical learning for Stage 5 learners (usually 9–10 years). It can be used as an independent resource for anyone wanting to encourage mathematical learning in children, or as a supplementary part of the *Cambridge Primary Mathematics* series.

If used as part of the series alongside the *Teacher's Resource 5* (9781107658547), then you will often be going directly to a specific game and page number according to the reference in the '*More activities*' section in the *Teacher's Resource* and will therefore already be familiar with the learning outcome of the game. If you are using the book as an independent resource, you can use the Objective map on the CD-ROM to help you determine what game you might want to play according to what learning outcome you are after, or you can simply read the '*Maths focus*' at the start of each game to decide if it's appropriate.

The games are grouped by strand, i.e. 'Number', 'Geometry', 'Measure' and 'Handling data' so that an independent user can easily navigate the pool of games. For those of you using this book alongside the *Teacher's Resource 5*, you will find that the games within a strand are ordered according to the order in which they are referenced in the *Teacher's Resource 5* (if you grouped all chapters of a given strand together).

Please note that the *Games Book* on its own does **not** cover all of the Cambridge Primary mathematics curriculum framework for Stage 5.

All games boards, game cards and record sheets provided within the printed book are also available on the CD-ROM for quick printing if preferred. Some games boards and resources will also be provided as Word documents so that you can adapt them as required. The CD-ROM also provides child-friendly instructions for each game, which can be displayed at the front of the class or sent home with the games for independent play. Nets for making dice, spinners and other useful mathematical resources are also provided as printable PDFs on the CD-ROM.

 This publication is part of the *Cambridge Primary Maths* project. *Cambridge Primary Maths* is an innovative combination of curriculum and resources designed to support teachers and learners to succeed in primary mathematics through best-practice international maths teaching and a problem-solving approach.

Cambridge Primary Maths brings together the world-class Cambridge Primary mathematics curriculum from Cambridge International Examinations, high-quality publishing from Cambridge University Press and expertise in engaging online enrichment materials for the mathematics curriculum from NRICH.

Teachers have access to an online tool that maps resources and links to materials offered through the primary mathematics curriculum, NRICH and Cambridge Primary mathematics textbooks and e-books. These resources include engaging online activities, best-practice guidance and examples of *Cambridge Primary Maths* in action.

The Cambridge curriculum is dedicated to helping schools develop learners who are confident, responsible, reflective, innovative and engaged. It is designed to give learners the skills to problem solve effectively, apply mathematical knowledge and develop a holistic understanding of the subject.

The *Cambridge Primary Maths* textbooks provide best-in-class support for this problem-solving approach, based on pedagogical practice found in successful schools across the world. The engaging NRICH online resources help develop mathematical thinking and problem-solving skills. To get involved visit www.cie.org.uk/cambridgeprimarymaths

The benefits of being part of *Cambridge Primary Maths* are:
- the opportunity to explore a maths curriculum founded on the values of the University of Cambridge and best practice in schools
- access to an innovative package of online and print resources that can help bring the Cambridge Primary mathematics curriculum to life in the classroom.

This series is arranged to ensure that the curriculum is covered whilst allowing teachers to use a flexible approach. The Scheme of Work for Stage 5 has been followed, though not in the same order and there will be some deviations. The components are:
- Teacher's Resource 5 ISBN: 9781107658547 (printed book and CD-ROM).
- Learner's Book 5 ISBN: 9781107638228 (printed book)
- Games Book 5 ISBN: 9781107614741 (printed book and CD-ROM).

For associated NRICH activities, please visit the *Cambridge Primary Maths* project at www.cie.org.uk/cambridgeprimarymaths

Remove a digit

Maths focus: understanding place value of numbers with up to six digits.

A game for two players

> **You will need:**
> - Game board (page 2).
> - A 1–6 dice (CD-ROM).
> - A different coloured counter (or alternative) for each player.

How to play
1. Both players place their counters on square 1, marked on the game board.
2. Players take turns to roll the dice and move forward that number of spaces on the game board.
3. If a player lands on a shaded square with a number displayed in large print, the player checks to see if the number contains a digit that matches their dice score. If it does, the player performs one subtraction to change the digit to zero. The player then moves forward the number on the dice again.
4. If a player lands on an unshaded square, or if the number on the game board does not contain a digit that matches the number on the dice, play passes to the other player.
5. Players may challenge an incorrect calculation. If the calculation is incorrect, the player misses their next turn.
6. The winner is the first player to reach or pass square 64.

Example: 3456 on the square and 5 on the dice.
The 5 is in the tens place, so we need to subtract 5 tens (50) to reduce the tens digit to zero.

The counting game

Maths focus: counting on and back in 1000s, 100s, and 10s in order to add and subtract.

A game for two or three players

> **You will need:**
> - Game board (page 3).
> - A set of 0–9 digit cards (CD-ROM).
> - A 1–6 dice (CD-ROM).
> - A different coloured counter (or alternative) for each player.

How to play
1. All players place their counters on 'Start'.
2. Each player takes three of the 1–9 digit cards. They arrange the cards to make any three-digit number, which they write at the top of their column of the grid.
3. Players take turns to throw the dice and move their counter around the board. They add or subtract according to the instructions on the spaces they land on and write their new number in their column.
4. Where the path goes in two directions players can choose which way to go.
5. Once all players have reached the finish, the player with the score closest to 3000 is the winner.

57	58	59	60	61	62	63	64
		4562			123 456		
56	55	54	53	52	51	50	49
3456			36 214			246 135	
41	42	43	44	45	46	47	48
	23 651			35			654 321
40	39	38	37	36	35	34	33
		241 365			563 412		
25	26	27	28	29	30	31	32
34 561			12 546			3612	
24	23	22	21	20	19	18	17
	126 543			36 152			4321
9	10	11	12	13	14	15	16
		531 246			54 123		
8	7	6	5	4	3	2	1
3654			43 512			164	

Player 1	Player 2	Player 3
Finish number	Finish number	Finish number

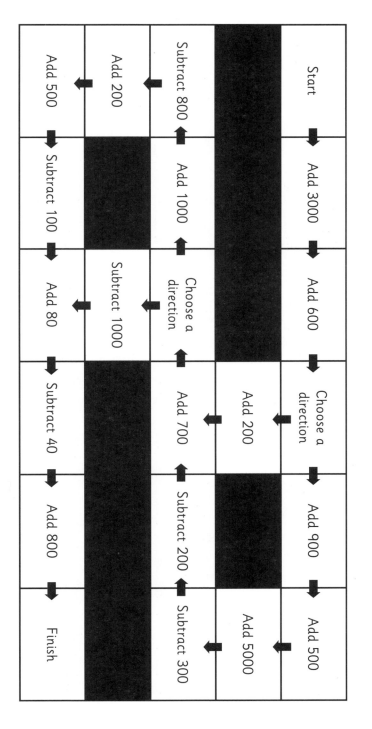

Start

Add 3000

Add 600

Choose a direction

Add 900

Add 500

Add 1000

Add 200

Add 700

Add 5000

Subtract 800

Choose a direction

Subtract 200

Subtract 300

Add 200

Subtract 1000

Add 800

Add 500

Subtract 100

Add 80

Subtract 40

Finish

Making 100

Maths focus: finding the total of more than three two-digit numbers using a written method.

A game for two or more players

You will need:
- A game card for each player (page 5).
- A 1–6 dice.

How to play

1. Each player needs a game card for adding four two-digit numbers.
2. Players take turns to throw the dice. After each throw all players write the number on the dice into one of the boxes on their card. Continue until all the boxes for are full.
3. Each player adds their two-digit numbers together, using which ever method they find reliable and efficient, and writes down their total.
4. The player whose total is closest to 100 is the winner.

Making 1000

Maths focus: Finding the total of more than three three-digit numbers using a written method.

A game for two or more players

You will need:
- A game card for each player (page 6).
- A 1–6 dice.

How to play

1. Each player needs a game card for adding four three-digit numbers.
2. Players take turns to throw the dice. After each throw all players write the number on the dice into one of the boxes on their card. Continue until all the boxes are full.
3. Each player adds their three-digit numbers together, using which ever method they find reliable and efficient, and writes down their total.
4. The player whose total is closest to 1000 is the winner.

Making 100 - Game cards

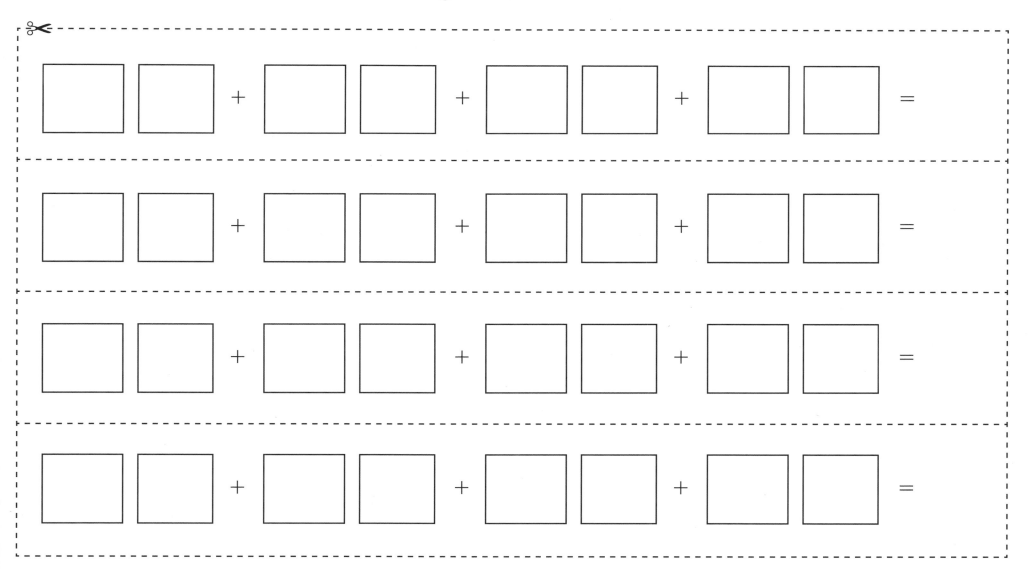

Making 1000 - Game cards

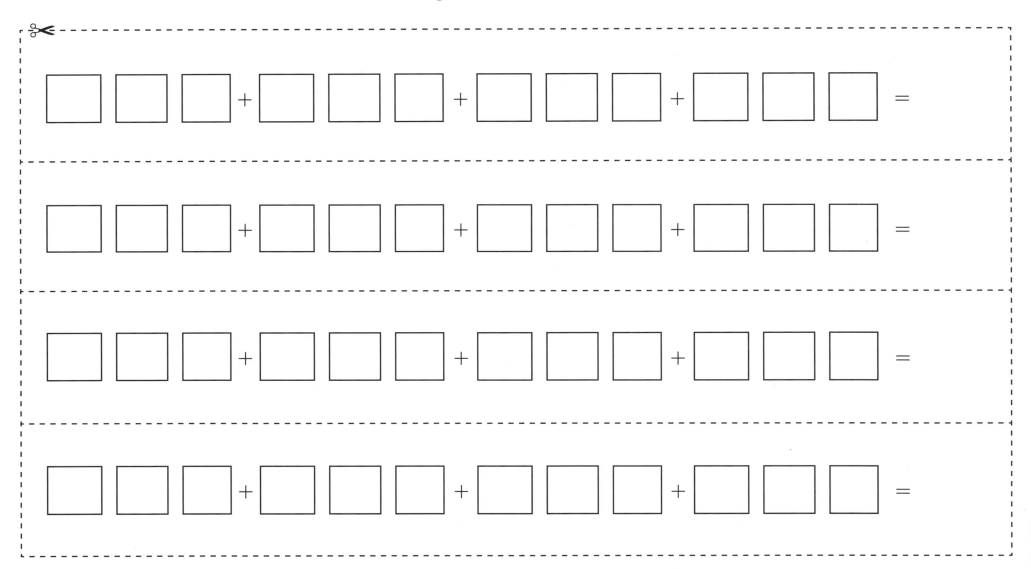

Multiplication bingo

Maths focus: revising multiplication facts to 10×10.

A game for a leader and up to 40 players

You will need:

For the leader:
- Game cards (page 8).
- A check sheet (uncut copy of the game cards).

For each player:
- A game board (pages 9–13).
- 15 counters.

How to play

1. The leader shuffles the game cards, then calls out one question at a time.
2. Each card can be read in different ways.

   For example, 3×8 can be read as:

3 times 8	8 times 3
3 multiplied by 8	8 multiplied by 3
the product of 3 and 8	the product of 8 and 3.

3. As each question is used, the leader places the game card on top of the matching question on the check sheet.
4. Players who have the answer on their game board cover it with a counter.
5. The first player to cover all their answers shouts 'Bingo' and is the winner. The leader checks the winner's game board by comparing the numbers on the board with the cards placed on the check sheet.

Square numbers

Maths focus: recognising and finding square numbers to 10×10.

A game for two players

You will need:
- Game board (page 14).
- A 1–10 spinner (CD-ROM).
- 20 counters (ten of one colour and ten of a different colour).

How to play

1. Players take turns to spin the spinner, square the number and choose a hexagon on the game board that contains their number.
2. The player places a counter over their chosen square number.
3. The first player to place four of their counters in a row – horizontally or diagonally – is the winner.

Multiplication bingo – Game cards

			2×2	2×3	2×4
2×5	2×6	2×7	2×8	2×9	2×10
3×3	3×4	3×5	3×6	3×7	3×8
3×9	3×10	4×4	4×5	4×6	4×7
4×8	4×9	4×10	5×5	5×6	5×7
5×8	5×9	5×10	6×6	6×7	6×8
6×9	6×10	7×7	7×8	7×9	7×10
8×8	8×9	8×10	9×9	9×10	10×10

Multiplication bingo – Game boards

4	6	16	18	21
24	28	32	35	42
45	56	63	81	100

6	9	10	18	21
24	28	30	32	42
45	56	64	81	100

6	9	16	18	20
25	28	32	35	42
48	50	63	70	81

4	9	15	16	20
21	28	30	35	45
49	56	63	70	81

6	8	14	18	20
27	28	32	36	42
48	60	64	72	80

4	9	12	15	21
24	25	30	32	45
49	54	64	72	80

4	6	10	16	20
25	28	35	36	42
45	50	56	72	90

8	9	12	14	24
25	27	32	35	40
49	54	63	81	100

6	8	10	18	24
27	28	30	35	42
45	56	63	81	100

4	6	15	16	21
24	27	32	36	42
48	60	64	70	81

8	9	10	14	20
21	28	30	36	42
48	60	64	70	81

4	8	15	16	24
27	28	30	32	45
49	50	56	72	90

6	9	14	18	21
24	27	32	35	40
49	54	63	81	100

6	8	12	14	20
24	27	32	35	48
49	54	64	72	90

4	9	10	16	24
25	28	30	35	42
48	50	63	72	80

4	8	12	15	20
25	27	32	35	40
49	50	63	72	90

6	9	12	15	20
27	28	30	32	45
49	54	63	72	90

6	8	15	16	21
24	25	32	35	40
42	60	64	70	81

4	9	10	18	24
25	27	32	36	42
48	56	63	81	100

4	6	14	18	24
27	28	35	36	42
45	50	56	72	80

4	9	16	18	21
24	27	32	35	42
48	50	56	72	80

6	8	12	15	24
25	28	30	35	42
45	54	63	72	90

8	9	15	16	21
24	28	30	32	45
49	54	64	70	81

4	6	10	18	20
25	27	32	36	48
49	50	63	81	100

4	8	14	18	20
21	24	32	35	40
49	60	64	70	81

6	9	10	16	20
27	28	30	35	42
48	50	56	72	80

8	9	14	18	24
25	28	35	36	45
49	50	56	72	80

4	8	10	16	20
25	27	30	32	42
48	54	63	72	90

6	8	16	18	20
21	28	32	35	45
49	56	63	70	81

4	9	12	14	20
25	28	32	36	42
45	54	63	72	90

6	8	16	18	24
25	27	32	35	45
48	50	63	81	100

8	9	10	18	20
25	28	30	32	48
49	50	56	72	90

4	6	12	15	20
25	28	35	36	45
49	54	64	70	81

8	9	10	18	21
24	25	32	36	42
45	56	63	72	80

6	9	14	18	20
25	28	32	36	42
48	50	63	72	90

4	9	12	14	21
24	28	30	35	42
45	54	64	81	100

4	8	10	16	21
24	25	35	36	48
49	56	63	81	100

4	8	15	16	24
25	27	30	35	42
45	54	63	72	80

4	6	12	15	20
27	28	32	36	42
48	60	64	72	80

6	9	12	14	24
27	28	30	32	45
49	60	64	70	81

Multiplication bingo – Game boards

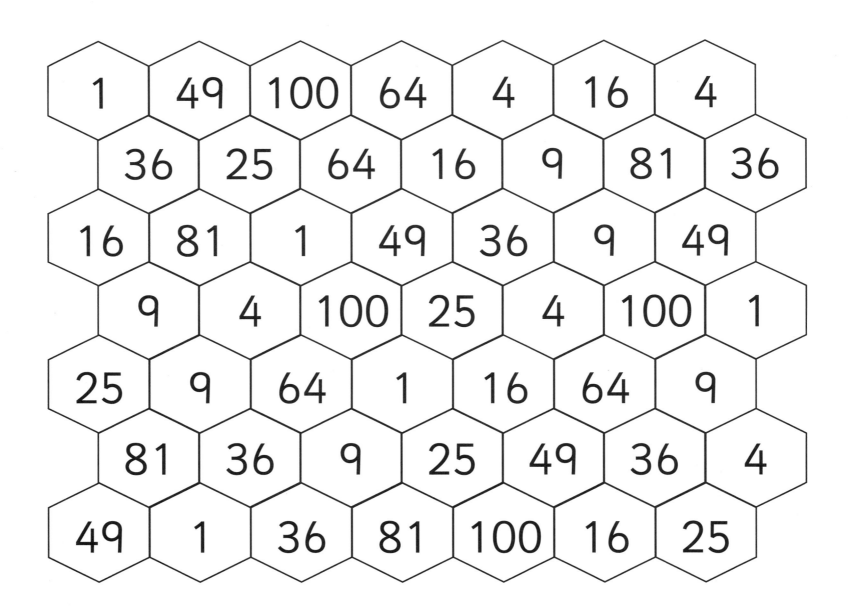

Square numbers – Game board

Sequences bingo

Maths focus: recognise and extend number sequences.

A game for a leader and up to 40 players

You will need:

For the leader:
- Game cards (page 16–17).
- A check sheet (uncut copy of Game cards).

For each player:
- A game board (reuse the boards from *Multiplication bingo*, page 9–13).
- 15 counters.

How to play

1. The leader shuffles the game cards, then calls out one question at a time. The bold number to the left of the sequence is the answer, so make sure the players cannot see the game cards or the check sheet.
2. As each question is asked, the leader ticks it off on their 'check sheet', so that they know what 'answer' numbers should have been ticked on the bingo boards.
3. Players who have the answer on their game board tick it off or colour it in.
4. The first player to tick all the numbers on their board shouts 'Bingo' and is the winner.
5. The leader checks the winner's game board by comparing the numbers on the board with the ticks placed on the check sheet.

Sailing boats

Maths focus: rounding a number with one decimal place to the nearest whole number.

A game for two players

You will need:
- Game boards (page 18).
- Two 0–9 spinners (CD-ROM).
- 10 coloured counters for each player.

How to play

1. Players take turns to roll both dice and make a number with one decimal place.
2. Example: *With a roll of 3 and 7, a player could make 3.7 or 7.3*
3. The player rounds their number to the nearest whole number and places a counter on the corresponding boat on their game board.
4. The winner is the first player to cover all their boats with a counter.

Challenge

Play the same game but with three 0-9 spinners. Players make a number with two decimal places, e.g. 3.65 with a 3, 6, and 5, and round it to the nearest whole number, which they cover on their corresponding boat.

Sequences bingo – Game cards

	4 Find the next number in this sequence: −12, −8, −4, 0, ☐	**6** Find the next number in this sequence: 30, 24, 18, 12, ☐
8 Find the missing number in this sequence: −10, −4, 2, ☐, 14	**9** Find the missing number in this sequence: −3, 3, ☐, 15, 21	**10** Find the next number in this sequence: 70, 55, 40, 25, ☐
12 Find the missing number in this sequence: 3, 6, ☐, 24, 48	**14** Find the missing number in this sequence: 7, ☐, 21, 28, 35	**15** Find the missing number in this sequence: 120, 60, 30, ☐, 7.5
16 Find the next number in this sequence: 4, 7, 10, 13, ☐	**18** Find the next number in this sequence: 54, 45, 36, 27, ☐	**20** Find the missing number in this sequence: 160, 80, 40, ☐, 10
21 Find the next number in this sequence: −19, −9, 1, 11, ☐	**24** Find the missing number in this sequence: 3, 6, 12, ☐, 48	**25** Find the missing number in this sequence: 625, 125, ☐, 5
27 Find the next number in this sequence: 15, 18, 21, 24, ☐	**28** Find the missing number in this sequence: 7, 14, 21, ☐, 35	**30** Find the next number in this sequence: 90, 75, 60, 45, ☐
32 Find the next number in this sequence: 2, 4, 8, 16, ☐	**35** Find the next number in this sequence: 63, 56, 49, 42, ☐	**36** Find the missing number in this sequence: 9, 18, ☐, 72, 144
40 Find the missing number in this sequence: 5, 10, 20, ☐, 80	**42** Find the next number in this sequence: 14, 21, 28, 35, ☐	**45** Find the next number in this sequence: 9, 18, 27, 36, ☐

48	Find the missing number in this sequence: 6, 12, 24, □, 96	**49**	Find the next number in this sequence: 21, 28, 35, 42, □	**50**	Find the next number in this sequence: −30, −10, 10, 30, □
54	Find the next number in this sequence: 18, 27, 36, 45, □	**56**	Find the next number in this sequence: 24, 32, 40, 48, □	**60**	Find the missing number in this sequence: 480, 240, 120, □, 30
63	Find the next number in this sequence: 99, 90, 81, 72, □	**64**	Find the next number in this sequence: 4, 8, 16, 32, □	**70**	Find the next number in this sequence: 350, 280, 210, 140, □
72	Find the missing number in this sequence: 54, 63, □, 81, 90	**80**	Find the next number in this sequence: 5, 10, 20, 40, □	**81**	Find the missing number in this sequence: 63, 72, □, 90, 99
90	Find the next number in this sequence: 10, 30, 50, 70, □	**100**	Find the next number in this sequence: −20, 10, 40, 70, □		

Sailing boats - Game boards

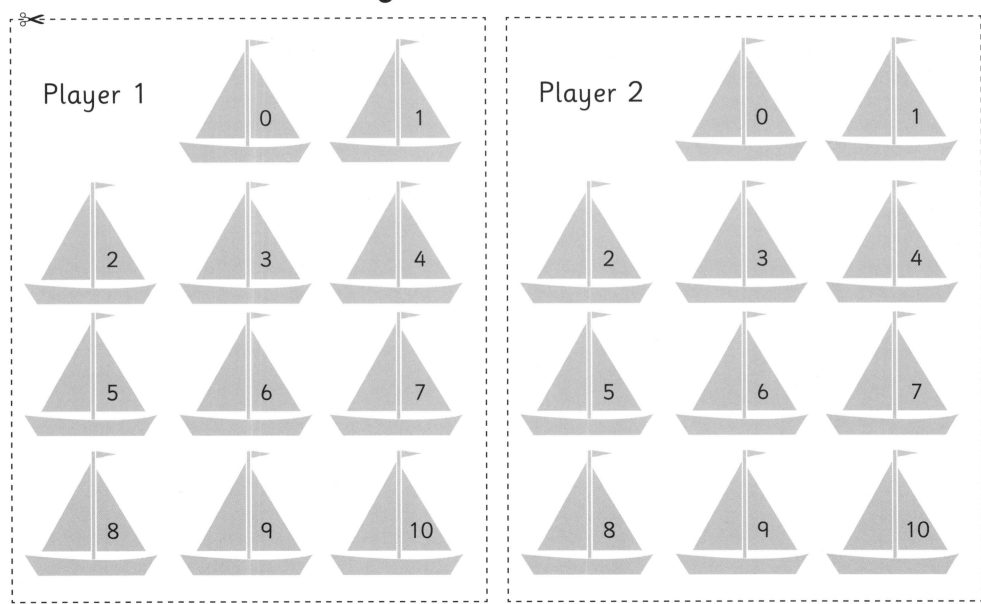

Product pairs

Maths focus: recalling multiplication facts to 10 × 10.

A game for two players

You will need:
- Game board (page 20).
- A set of 1–10 digit cards (CD-ROM).

How to play
1. Spread the digit cards face down on the table.
2. Players take turns to pick a card and write the number anywhere on their own grid.
3. After four goes, each grid will contain four numbers.
4. Each player decides how to pair their numbers.
5. Each player writes down the product of each pair and the total of the two products.
   Example:

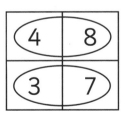 *or*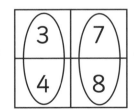

   24 + 28 = 52 *or* 12 + 56 = 68

6. The player with the largest total wins the round.
7. Play continues for a set time or a set number of rounds.

The difference game

Maths focus: calculating differences between near multiples of 1000, e.g. 5026 – 4998.

A game for two or more players

You will need:
- Game board (page 21).
- Game cards (page 22) copied onto card and cut out.

How to play
1. Each player takes their game board. They should see that it is for subtraction of two four-digit numbers.
2. Shuffle the number cards and place them face down in a pile.
3. Turn over one card. All players write the digit in one space on their game board.
4. Cards are turned over one at a time and digits are placed after each card is turned over. Once a digit has been placed it cannot be moved.
5. Once eight digits have been placed players carry out their subtraction. If a player has a second number greater than their first number they are out of the game.
6. The player with the greatest difference is the winner.

Product pairs – Game boards

Total

☐ + ☐ = ☐

Total

☐ + ☐ = ☐

Total

☐ + ☐ = ☐

The difference game – Game boards

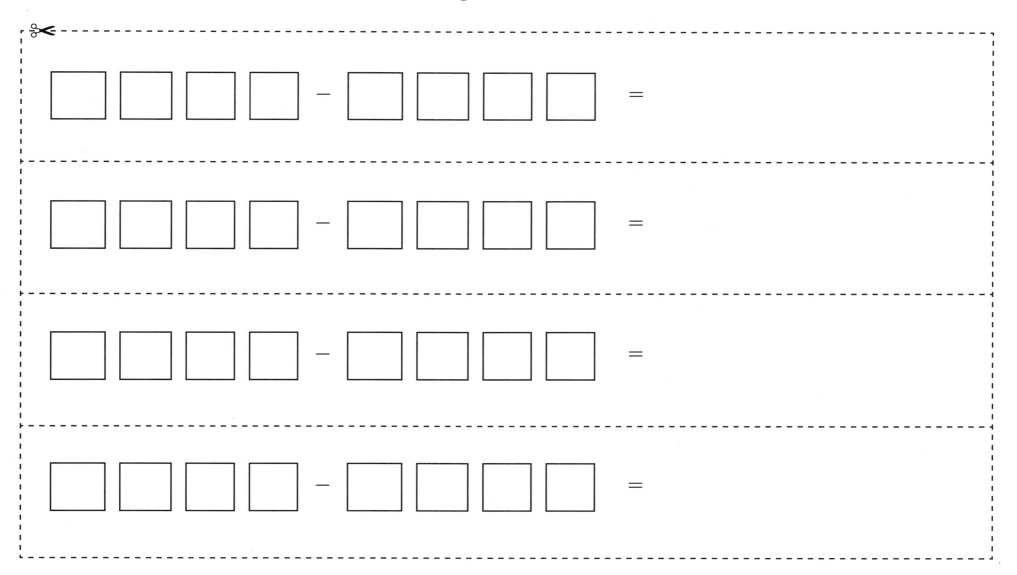

The difference game – Game cards

0	0	0	0
0	0	0	0
1	1	1	1
1	1	1	1
8	8	8	8
8	8	8	8
9	9	9	9
9	9	9	9

The money game

Maths focus: adding or subtracting any pair of three and/or four-digit numbers, with the same number of decimal places, including amounts of money.

A game for two or more players

You will need:
- Game board (page 24).
- Game cards (page 25) (If necessary change '$' to the local unit of currency.)
- A dice.
- A timer (e.g. kitchen timer, stopwatch or clock) for timing 10 minutes.

How to play
1. Shuffle the cards and place them face down in a pile in the 'cards' space on the board.
2. Players start with a total of $100. They start the timer and take turns to throw the dice and move around the board, adding or subtracting according to the instructions on the spaces they land on.
3. Play continues until the 10-minute time limit is reached. Any player who runs out of money during the 10 minutes is out of the game.
4. The player with the greatest amount of money at the end of the game is the winner.

Find your answer – multiplication

Maths focus: finding the product of a three-digit number and a single-digit number.

A game for two players

You will need:
- Game board (page 26).
- 20 counters (ten of one colour and ten of a different colour).
- Paper for jottings.

How to play
1. Players each take a set of counters.
2. Player 1 chooses one number from group A on the game board and one number from group B and multiplies them together.
3. The player places a counter over the answer if it appears on the grid. If the number does not appear on the grid, the player misses a go.
4. Player 2 has a turn.
5. The winner is the first player to have four counters in a row – vertically, horizontally or diagonally.

Start or have a rest! →	Spend $2.90 on lunch →	Miss a turn →	Pick up a card →	Give $10 to charity. Well done →	Find an extra $10 in your money box!
Pick up a card ↑			**Cards**		Pick up a card ↓
Spend $1.25 on bus fare ↑					Spend $1.25 on bus fare ↓
Pick up a card ↑					Miss a turn ↓
Find an extra $10 in your money box! ←	Give $10 to charity. Well done ←	Pick up a card ←	Win $20 in a mathematics competition ←	Spend $2.90 on lunch ←	Pick up a card ↓

The money game – Game cards

Birthday! Give one other player $10.50	Birthday! Give one other player $7.25	Birthday! Give one other player $9.75	Birthday! Give one other player $12.95
Shopping Pay $14.78	**Shopping** Pay $24.07	**Shopping** Pay $9.22	**Shopping** Pay $5.38
Shopping Pay $10.65	**Shopping** Pay $2.06	**Shopping** Pay $15.49	**Shopping** Pay $8.80
Gift Receive $3.48	**Gift** Receive $9.04	**Gift** Receive $16.14	**Gift** Receive $12.60
Entertainment Pay $5.99	**Entertainment** Pay $17.28	**Entertainment** Pay $13.83	**Entertainment** Pay $20.41
Chores Get paid $10.89	**Chores** Get paid $15.09	**Chores** Get paid $8.27	**Chores** Get paid $6.20

5	8	4
6	7	9

719	929	372
436	428	874

		3595	4314	2996	1488		
2876	7866	5244	1712	3488	5752	5033	2140
3348	2604	7432	3852	6503	4645	1744	2616
6471	6992	2180	3496	6118	8361	2976	2568
4370	3716	3052	3924	5574	3424	2232	1860

Find your answer – division

Maths focus: finding the result of dividing a three-digit number by a single-digit number.

A game for two players

You will need:
- Game board (page 28).
- 20 counters (ten of one colour ten of a different colour).
- Paper for working out.
- Calculator for checking (optional).

How to play

1. Players each take a set of counters.
2. Player 1 chooses one number from group A on the game board and one number from group B, then divides the number in group B by the number in group A.
3. The player places a counter over the answer if it appears on the grid. If the number does not appear on the grid, the player misses a go.
4. Player 2 has a turn.
5. The winner is the first player to have four counters in a row – vertically, horizontally or diagonally.

Double, halve or stick?

Maths focus: practising doubling and halving two-digit numbers mentally.

A game for two to four players

You will need:
- Two spinners (page 30).
- Pencil and paperclip to make the spinner.
- Recording sheet (optional, see page 29).

How to play

1. Player 1 sets a target number, for example 30. Players take turns to spin both spinners and say the number shown, for example 84.
2. The aim is for players to make their number as close to the target number as possible. To do this, they can choose to: double their number (D); halve their number (H) or stick with their number (S).
3. Each player performs the calculation either mentally or with the aid of jottings. If the answer includes a half, then players round up to the next whole number.
4. Players check all the results and the player with the number closest to the target number wins 4 points, the next closest 3 points and so on. The winner chooses the next target number and the game continues for a specified time or until a player wins a specified number of points.
5. The winner is the player with the most points.

Example game:

Name	Spinner score	Decision D / H / S	Difference	Score
Conrad	28	S = 28	2	4
Magda	65	H = 32.5 → 33	3	3

Group A

5	8	4
6	7	3

Group B

126	336	180	216	144
140	168	364	210	280

Grid

70	35	91	42	60
45	84	27	52	21
28	42	112	72	40
24	56	48	18	36
20	28	54	35	30

Double, halve or stick? – recording sheets

Sheet 1

Name	Spinner score	Target Number ☐		
		Decision D / H / S	Difference	Score

Sheet 2

Name	Spinner score	Target Number ☐		
		Decision D / H / S	Difference	Score

Sheet 3

Name	Spinner score	Target Number ☐		
		Decision D / H / S	Difference	Score

Sheet 4

Name	Spinner score	Target Number ☐		
		Decision D / H / S	Difference	Score

Double, halve or stick? - spinner templates

What to do:

1. Cut out the spinners.
2. Lay a paper clip on the top of the spinner, so that the end of it lies at the centre of the spinner.
3. Hold the point of a pencil through the hole in the end of the paper clip so that the tip of the pencil is on the centre of the spinner.
4. Hold the pencil firmly and spin around to generate numbers.

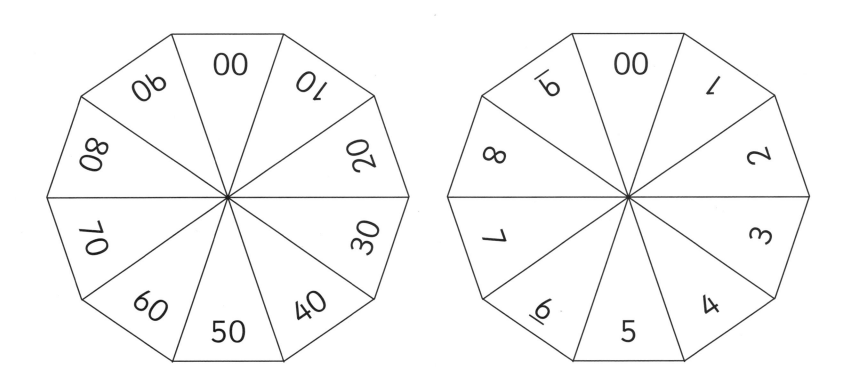

Less than

Maths focus: ordering numbers with one or two decimal places using < signs.

A game for two to four players

You will need:
- Game cards copied onto card and cut out (page 32).

How to play

1. Keep the '10 < ' cards separate from the main pack.
2. Shuffle the remaining cards. Deal seven cards to each player and place the rest face down in a pile.
3. Place a '10 <' card on the table. Players take turns to lay a card, either to the left or right of the cards on the table, making a correct sequence. Example –

1.16 <	1.6 <	10 <	11.7 <

4. If a player cannot add any of their cards to either end of the sequence they pick up a card from the pile and miss that turn.
5. When no players can go a new '10 < ' card is laid to start a new sequence.
6. The first player to have laid all of their cards is the winner.

Fraction and percentage dominoes

Maths focus: recognising equivalence between fractions and percentages

A game for two or four players

You will need:
- Game cards copied onto card and cut out (page 33).

How to play

1. Place the game cards face down on the table.
2. Each player chooses their game cards (five game cards each if there are four players and 10 game cards each if there are two players).
3. The player with the game card showing 100% places this on the table.
4. Players then take turns to match one side of the game card to the line of game cards played.

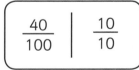  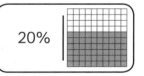

5. If a player is unable to go they miss that turn.
6. Play continues until one player has laid all their game cards.

Less than – Game cards

1.96 <	5.25 <	10.45 <	12	10 <
1.6 <	5.2 <	9.5 <	11.7 <	10 <
1.16 <	4.73 <	9.35 <	11.69 <	10 <
1.1 <	4.37 <	9.11 <	11.65 <	10 <
0.95 <	3.66 <	8.99 <	11.6 <	
0.77 <	3.6 <	7.5 <	10.88 <	
0.71 <	2.1 <	7.49 <	10.8 <	
0.54 <	2.01 <	6.66 <	10.75 <	
0.07 <	1.99 <	6.4 <	10.5 <	

Fraction and percentage dominoes – Game cards

$\frac{6}{10}$ 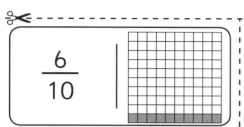	$\frac{10}{100}$ | $\frac{30}{100}$	30% 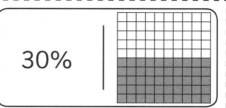	$\frac{50}{100}$ | $\frac{90}{100}$
90% | $\frac{60}{100}$	60% 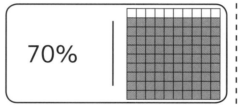	$\frac{8}{10}$ | $\frac{1}{2}$	50% | $\frac{1}{10}$
10% 	$\frac{3}{10}$ | $\frac{7}{10}$	70%	$\frac{9}{10}$ |
$\frac{100}{100}$ | $\frac{80}{100}$	80%	$\frac{2}{10}$ | $\frac{4}{10}$	40% 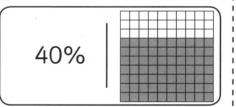
$\frac{70}{100}$	$\frac{40}{100}$ | $\frac{10}{10}$	100% | $\frac{20}{100}$	20%

Operation dice game

Maths focus: using mathematical operations including brackets if needed.

A game for two players

You will need:
- Game board (page 35).
- Three 1–6 dice (CD-ROM).
- Counters in two different colours.
- Whiteboards or paper (for working out).

How to play

1. Player 1 rolls the three dice and then uses all three numbers to make a number sentence that has an answer that is one of the numbers on the board. The player can use any operation sign or signs, together with brackets when needed.

Example: Player throws 2, 3, 4. The player creates the sequence: $(2 \times 3) + 4 = 10$, and places their counter on the number '10'. (Note that Player 1 could also have chosen $2 + 3 + 4 = 9$ and so on.)

2. Player 2 checks the calculation. If it is correct, Player 1 can leave their counter on the game board.
3. Player 2 rolls the dice and proceeds in the same way.
4. The winner is the first player to have four of their counters in a row – horizontally or diagonally.

The smoothie ratio game

Maths focus: using ratio to solve problems.

A game for two to four players

You will need:
- A game card for each player (page 36).
- Fruit cards (page 37).
- The Key card (page 37).
- A 1–6 dice (CD-ROM).

How to play

1. Shuffle the fruit cards and place them face down in a pile. Each player has the recipes for three fruit smoothies on their game card as ratios. Players create the smoothies by collecting the fruit cards to match the ratio on each glass. Each smoothie needs four or five fruit cards.

Example: Apple Zing, pineapple and apple 4 : 1, needs 4 pineapple cards and one apple card.

2. Players take turns to roll the dice. Each number on the dice corresponds to a fruit on the 'Key'. If the player needs the fruit that corresponds to their dice score for their smoothie they take one fruit card and place it in the appropriate glass. If they do not need that fruit, play passes to the next player.
3. The player who completes all three smoothies on their tray first is the winner.

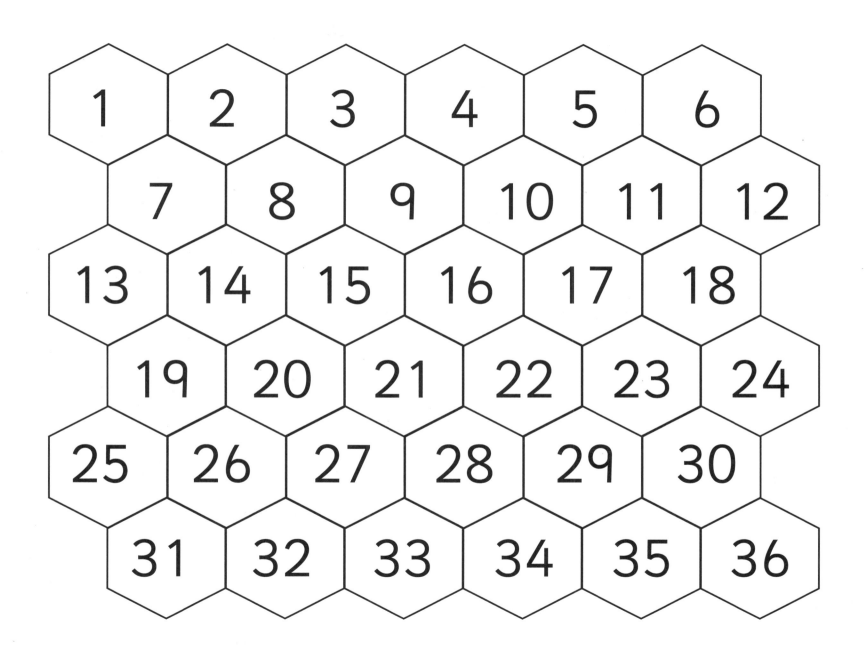

The smoothie ratio game – Game cards

Cosy Banana	**Tropical Dream**	**Berry Delight**
banana and apple	pineapple and kiwi fruit	strawberries and blueberries
3 : 1	1 : 4	3 : 2

Cosy Banana	**Tropical Dream**	**Turquoise Tipple**
banana and apple	pineapple and kiwi fruit	blueberries and kiwi fruit
3 : 1	1 : 4	4 : 1

Cosy Banana	**Apple Zing**	**Berry Delight**
banana and apple	pineapple and apple	strawberries and blueberries
3 : 1	4 : 1	3 : 2

Pink Drink	**Tropical Dream**	**Berry Delight**
banana and strawberry	pineapple and kiwi fruit	strawberries and blueberries
1 : 3	1 : 4	3 : 2

The smoothie ratio game – Key

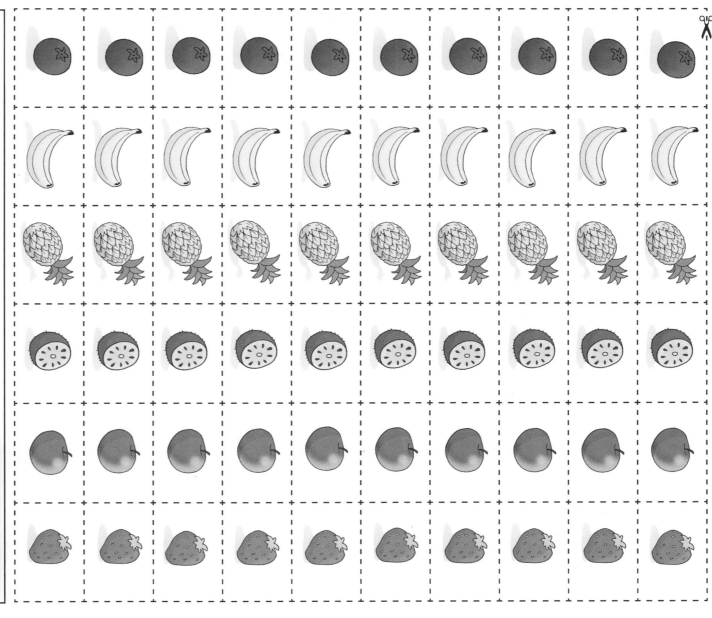

Key

1 = blueberry
2 = banana
3 = pineapple
4 = kiwi fruit
5 = apple
6 = strawberry

The smoothie ratio game – fruit cards

Perpendicular and parallel

Maths focus: recognising perpendicular and parallel lines in 2D shapes, drawings and the environment.

A game for two players

You will need:
- Game board (page 40).
- One coin.
- Two coloured pencils of different colours.
- A ruler.

How to play

1. Player 1 starts at the left side of the game board. Their aim is to make an unbroken line from the left side to the right side joining ◯ shapes. Player 2 starts at the top of the game board. Their aim is to make an unbroken line from the top to the bottom of the game board joining ■ shapes.
2. For their first turn each player can join any two of their shapes that are next to each other, with a vertical or horizontal line.
3. Players then take it in turns to flip a coin and draw a line on the board between **any** two of their shapes, so long as those shapes are next to each other; they do not have to be next to a previous line. They draw a line according to the following rules. If the coin lands showing:
   - a head, they draw a line perpendicular to any of their other lines.
   - tails, they draw a line parallel to any of their other lines.
4. The winner is the first player to make an unbroken line between their two sides.

The triangle picture game

Maths focus: identifying and describing properties of triangles and classifying them as isosceles, equilateral or scalene.

A game for two to four players

You will need:
- Game board (page 41).
- A 1–6 dice (CD-ROM).
- A game card (page 42) for each player.
- A counter for each player.
- Triangles (page 43) copied onto card and cut out.
- A box or tray to hold the triangle pieces.

How to play

1. Each player takes a game card. The triangles are placed in the box or tray near to the game board.
2. All players place their counters on 'Start' on the game board.
3. Players take turns to throw the dice and move that number of spaces in the direction of the arrows. They follow the instructions on the space where their counter lands, collecting the correct shape triangle from the box when directed to. If, for any reason, the player is unable to follow the instruction, play passes to the next player.
4. Players continue to throw the dice and move their counters around the outside of the board, following the direction of the arrows. Once a player has all the triangles necessary to build the picture shown on their picture card, they use their dice throws to follow the dotted arrows to the 'Finish' space.
5. The winner is the first player to reach the 'Finish' space with all the pieces for their picture.

Player 2 Top

Player 1 Left

Player 1 Right

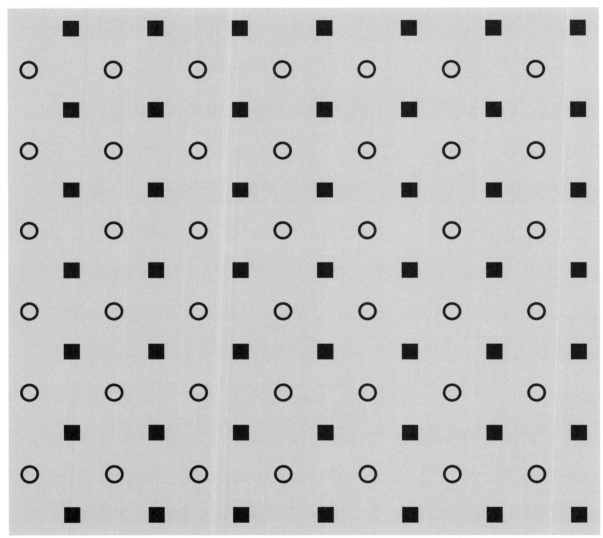

Player 2 Bottom

Heads
Draw a line **perpendicular** to a previous line.

Tails
Draw a line **parallel** to a previous line.

Example

Player 1 decides to start in the centre of the board. On turn 2 they flipped a coin and it showed tails, line (2) has to be parallel to the first line, so they have to draw a line somewhere else on the board and connect the two lines on another turn.

On player 1's next turn, they get a head, they draw a perpendicular line and join their other two lines up.

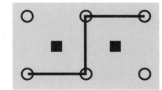

Start (or throw again) ➡	**Take 1 equilateral triangle** ➡	**Miss 1 turn** ➡	**Take 1 scalene triangle** ➡	**Go forward 3 spaces** ⬇
Take 1 isosceles triangle ⬆		**Go back 1 space** ⬇		**Take 1 isosceles triangle** ⬇
Go back 2 spaces ⬆	**Miss 1 turn** ▋▋➡	★ **Finish**	**Miss 1 turn** ⬅▋▋	**Go back 5 spaces** ⬇
Take 1 scalene triangle ⬆		**Go back 1 space** ⬆		**Take 1 equilateral triangle** ⬇
Put back 1 equilateral triangle ⬅	**Take 1 isosceles triangle** ⬅	**Miss 1 turn** ⬅	**Take 1 scalene triangle** ⬅	**Swap 1 triangle with another player** ⬅

The triangle picture game – Game cards

The cabin in the woods

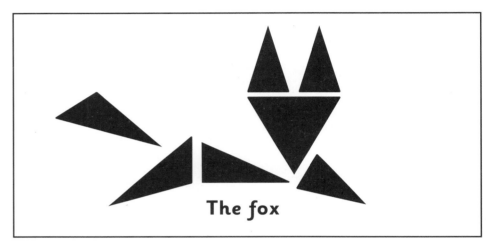

The fox

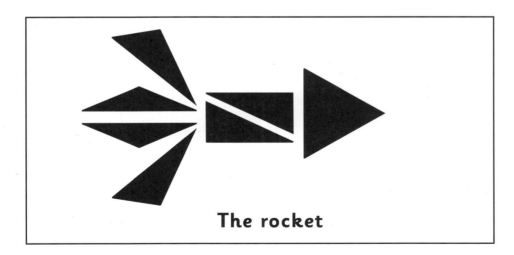

The rocket

The candles

The triangle picture game – Triangles

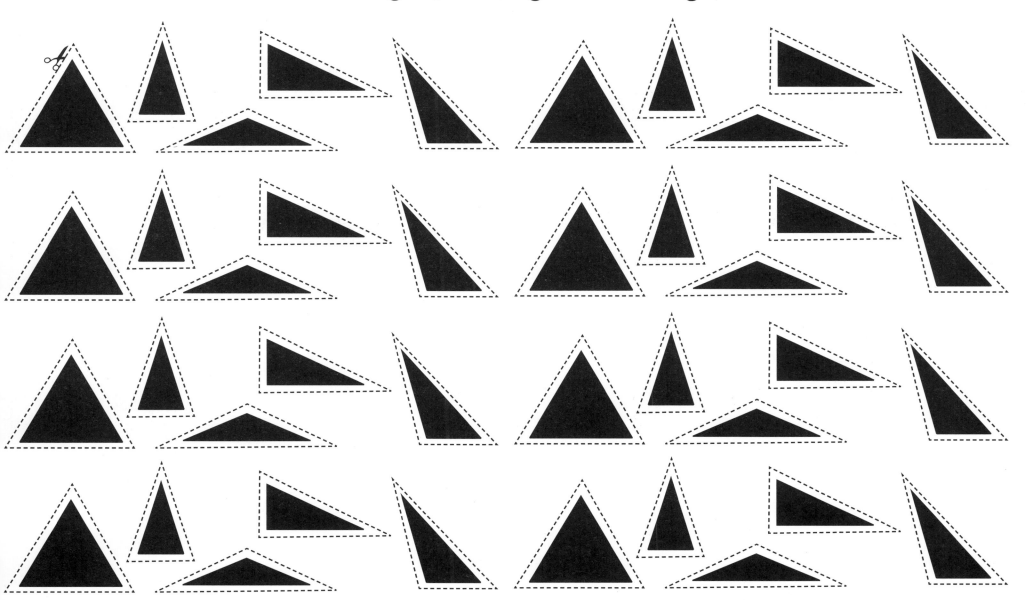

The cube picture game

Maths focus: visualising 3D shapes from 2D drawings.

A game for two players

You will need:
- 10 small cubes for each player.
- Game cards (page 45).

How to play

1. Each player takes 10 cubes. The cards are shuffled and placed in a pile face down on the table.
2. A player takes the top card, turns it over and places it on the table where both players can see it.
3. The players race to make the arrangement shown on the card with their 10 cubes.
4. The first player to make the arrangement takes the card.
5. The players turn over the next card in the pile and race to make the new arrangement.
6. The winner is the first person to collect four cards. There are three spare cards so that players can create their own arrangements to add to the set.

Three-in-a-row coordinates game

Maths focus: reading and plotting coordinates in the first quadrant.

A game for two players

You will need:
- Game board (page 46).
- Two sets of counters of different colours.
- Two 0–6 dice (CD-ROM).

How to play

1. Players take it in turn to roll the two dice. They use the numbers on the dice to make a coordinate which they write down in the table on the game board.

Example: If a 2 and a 6 are thrown, the player can make (2, 6) or (6, 2).

2. The player covers the coordinate they have made with one of their counters. If that position has already been covered by a counter (their own counter or that of their opponent) they miss a turn.
3. The winner is the first player to place three of their counters in a row – vertically, horizontally or diagonally.

The cube picture game – Game cards

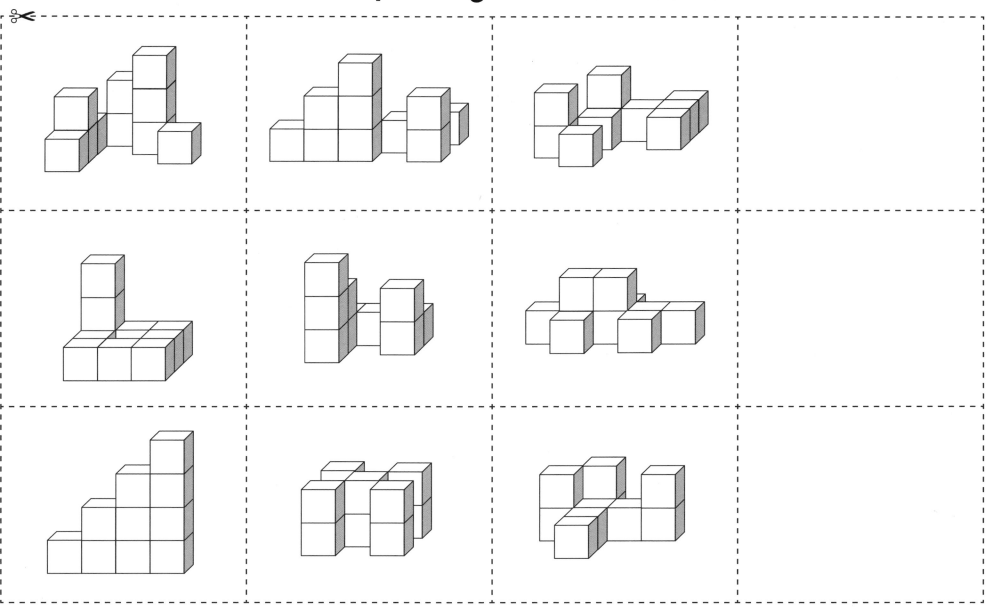

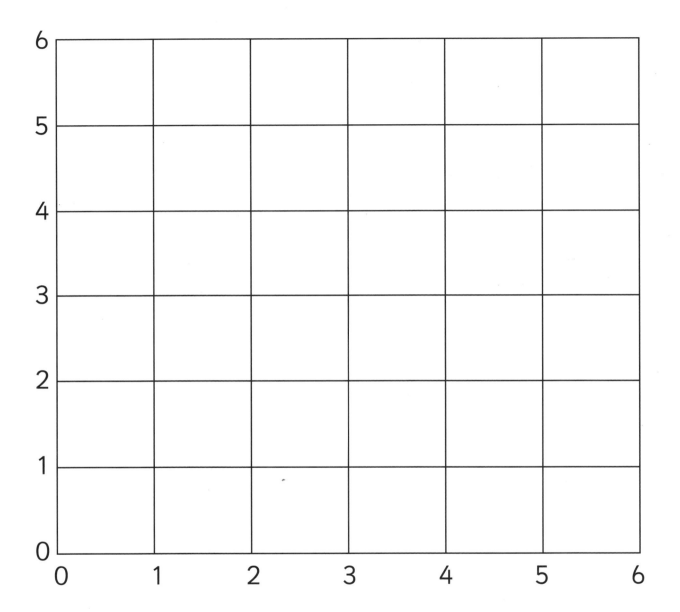

List of Coordinates

Player 1	Player 2

Three-in-a-row coordinates game – Game board

Translation swap

Maths focus: understanding translation as movement along a straight line.

A game for two players

You will need:
- Game board (page 48).
- Two different coloured counters (one for each player).
- Game cards (page 49).

How to play

1. Player 1 starts with their counter on position 1. Player 2 starts with their counter on position 2. Shuffle the game cards and place them face down, in a pile, on the table.
2. Players take it in turns to take a card. They follow the instruction on the card to move either their own counter or their opponent's counter along the lines of the board. If one of the counters can be moved using the instruction then the player must play their turn. If neither counter can be moved using the instruction on the card then play passes to the other player.
3. The winner is the first player to reach their opponent's starting position.

Estimating angles

Maths focus: understanding and using angle measure in degrees; identifying, describing and estimating the size of angles.

A game for two to four players

You will need:
- Game cards (page 50–52).
- 180° protractors / angle measurers.

How to play

1. Shuffle the game cards and place them face down, in a pile on the table. The first game card is turned over. Every player privately writes down an estimate. Each player measures the angle and they agree the angle to the nearest 5°. The player(s) with the closest estimate write down the true size of the angle.
2. Further game cards are turned over. Each time, the players estimate the size of the angle and measure the angle, and the players with the closest estimates add the size of the angle to the angles they have written down.
3. The first player to make a total of 360°, or over, is the winner.

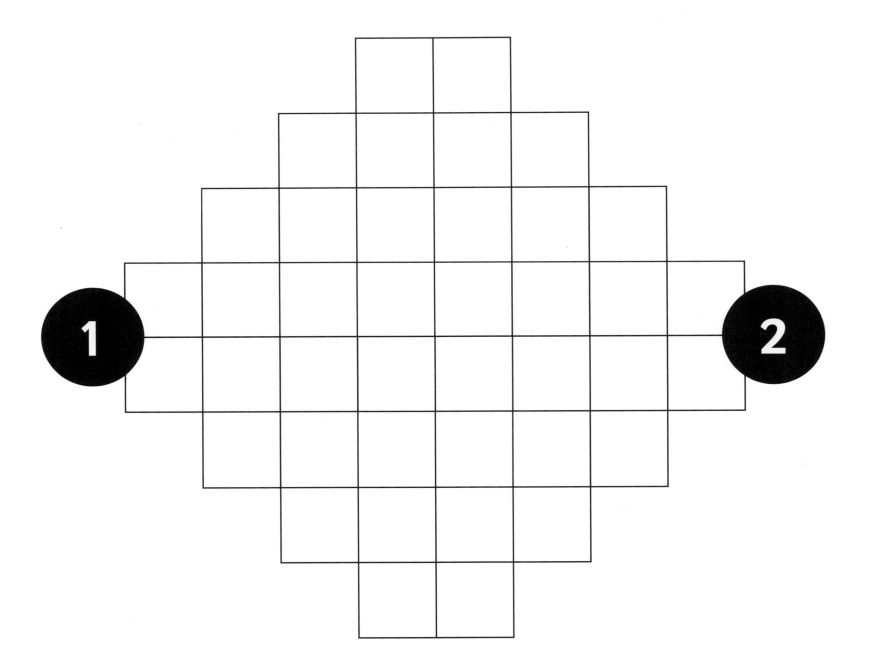

Translation swap – Game board

Translation swap – Game cards

1 left	2 left	3 left	4 left
1 right	2 right	3 right	4 right
1 up	2 up	3 up	4 up
1 down	2 down	3 down	4 down

Estimating angles – Game cards

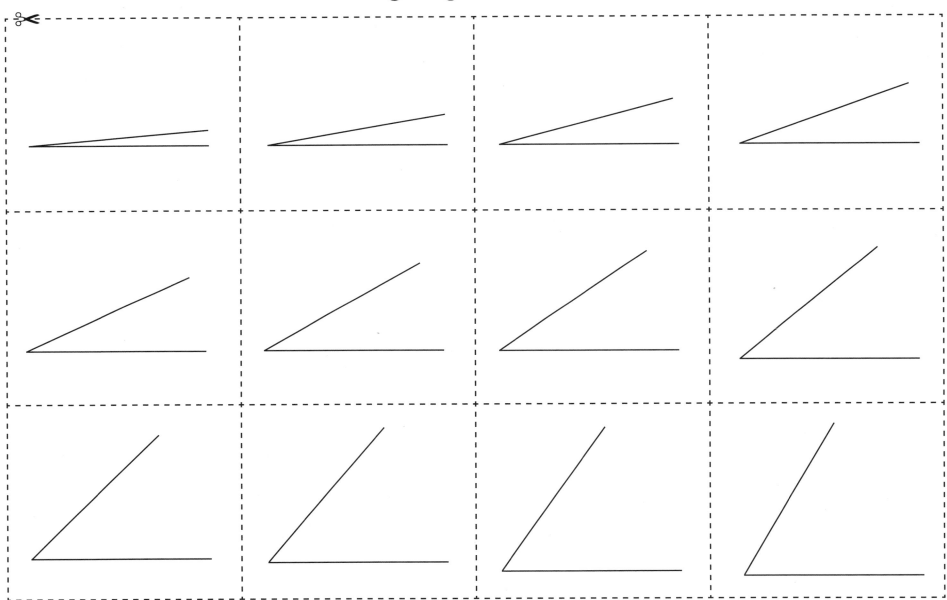

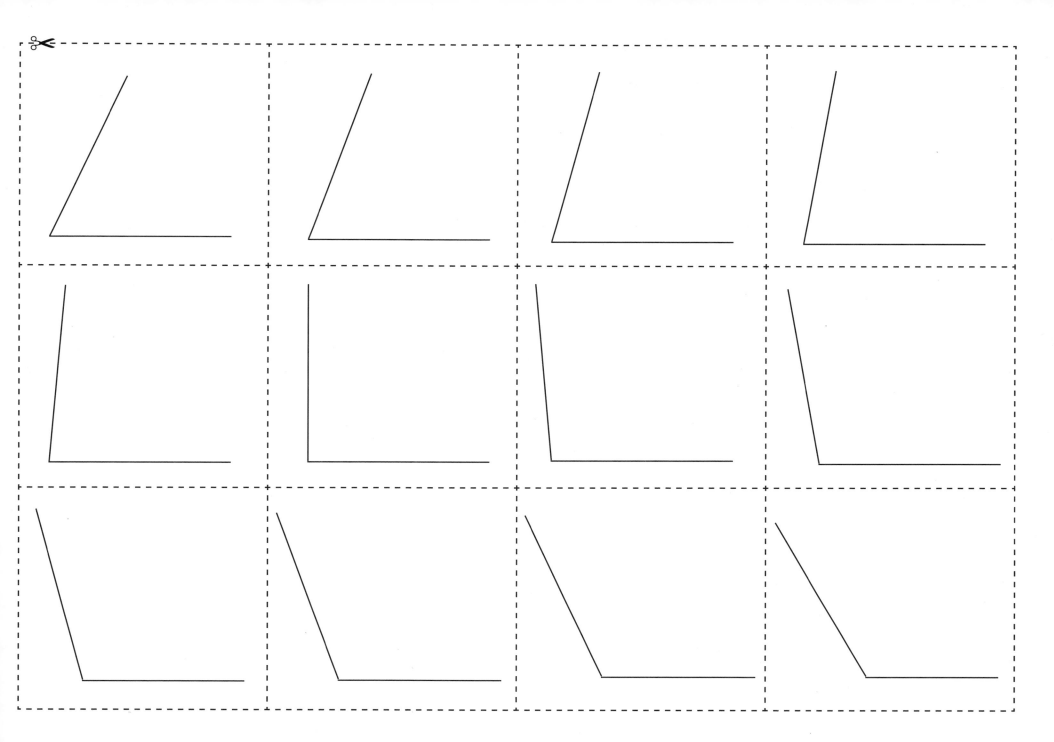

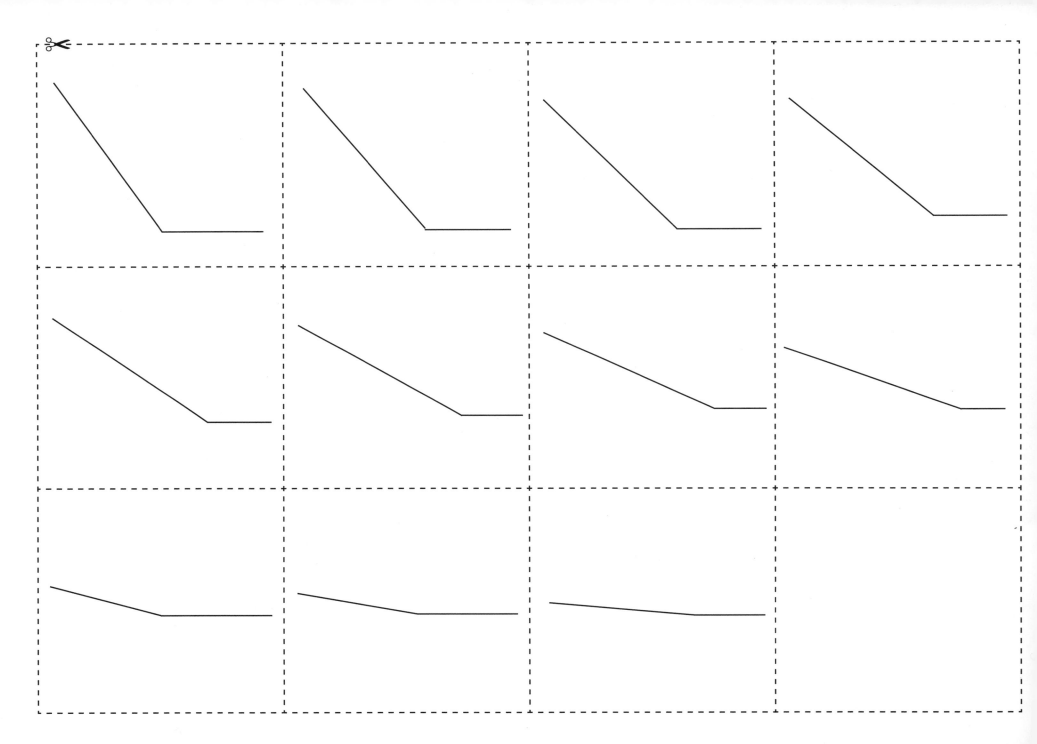

Triangle snap

Maths focus: identifying and describing properties of triangles and classifying them as isosceles, equilateral or scalene.

A game for two to four players

You will need:
• Game cards (page 54).

How to play

1. Shuffle the game cards and deal them out equally amongst the players. The players keep their cards in a pile, face down.
2. One player places the card from the top of their pile face up in the middle of the table.
3. The player to their left does the same. If the cards are a 'snap' (i.e. if they are the same type of triangle form the list below) players must call 'snap'. The first player to say 'snap' takes the cards and adds them to the bottom of their pile.
4. If a player runs out of cards they're out.
5. The last player in the game is the winner.

The six types of triangle in the game are:
• equilateral
• acute isosceles
• obtuse isosceles
• right-angled scalene
• acute scalene
• obtuse scalene

Note: two isosceles or scalene triangles are not a snap unless they are both acute or obtuse.

Four-in-a-row reflection game

Maths focus: visualising where an object will be after reflection over a mirror line.

A game for two players

You will need:
• Game board (page 55), or same grid drawn on squared paper.
• Two different coloured pencils, one for each player.
• One small mirror for checking the reflections.

How to play

1. Players take it in turns to colour in a square on their side of the game board. They can colour in any square they want so long as its reflection over the mirror line will not be in the same place as the reflection of any of their opponent's squares. They cannot colour in the reflection section, they must visualise the reflection.
2. The winner is the first player to successfully colour in a row of squares on their side of the game board. The row can be horizontal or vertical.
3. If there is accusation of overlapping squares, each player checks by visualising; if this cannot be agreed then they can colour in the reflection section. If there is overlap, the player whose square was there first is declared the winner, even if they do not have 4 in a row.
4. When one player believes they have successfully made a row of 4, both players colour in the reflection section by reflecting each of their squares in their mirror line. If the declaring player is correct, they win, if they are not, the other player automatically wins even if they have not got 4 in a row.
5. If 24 squares have been coloured on both sides of the board and no player has declared that they have a line of 4, the game is a draw.

Triangle snap – Game cards

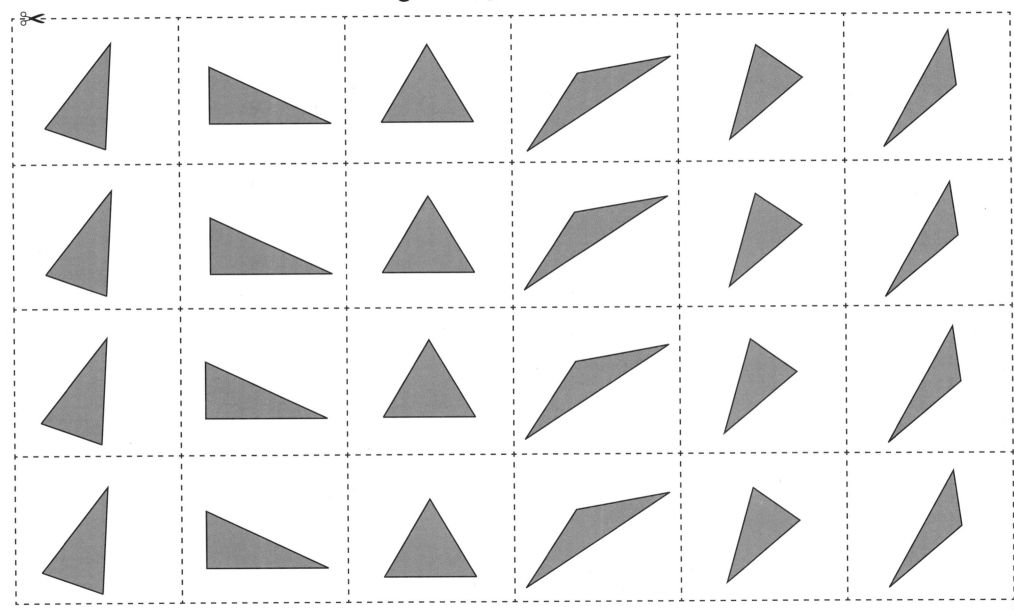

Player 1's board **Reflection** **Player 2's board**

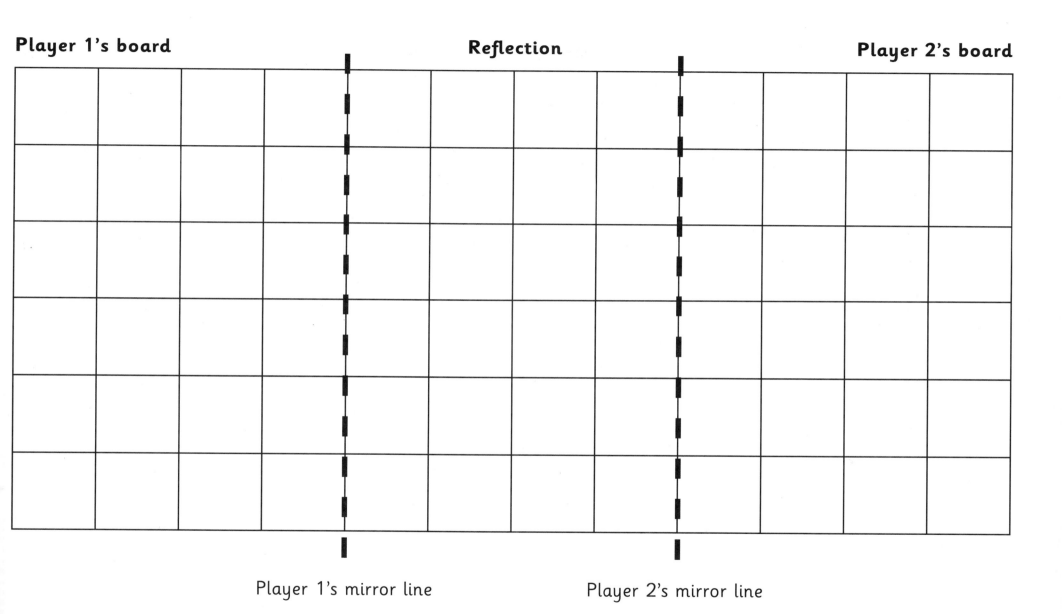

Player 1's mirror line   Player 2's mirror line

3D shape and net matching

Maths focus: visualising 3D shapes from 2D drawings and nets.

A game for two to four players

You will need:
- Game cards (page 57).

How to play
1. Shuffle the cards and spread them face down on a table.
2. Players take turns to turn over two cards in position. If the player turns over a shape and a net that match, the player keeps the two cards. If they do not match, then the player returns the cards face down.
3. The game ends when all the cards have been taken. The player who has taken the most cards is the winner.

The translation game

Maths focus: understanding translation as movement along a straight line, identifying where polygons will be after translation and giving instructions for translating shapes.

A game for two players

You will need:
- Game board (page 58).
- Two triangular player pieces (page 58).

How to play
1. Players take turns move their piece each −3, −2, −1, +1, +2, or +3 horizontally or vertically. They should say the type of translation they are making as they move their piece.
2. Players must move on each of their turns.
3. The winner is the player who moves their triangle so that it touches any part of the other player's triangle.

3D shape and net matching – Game cards

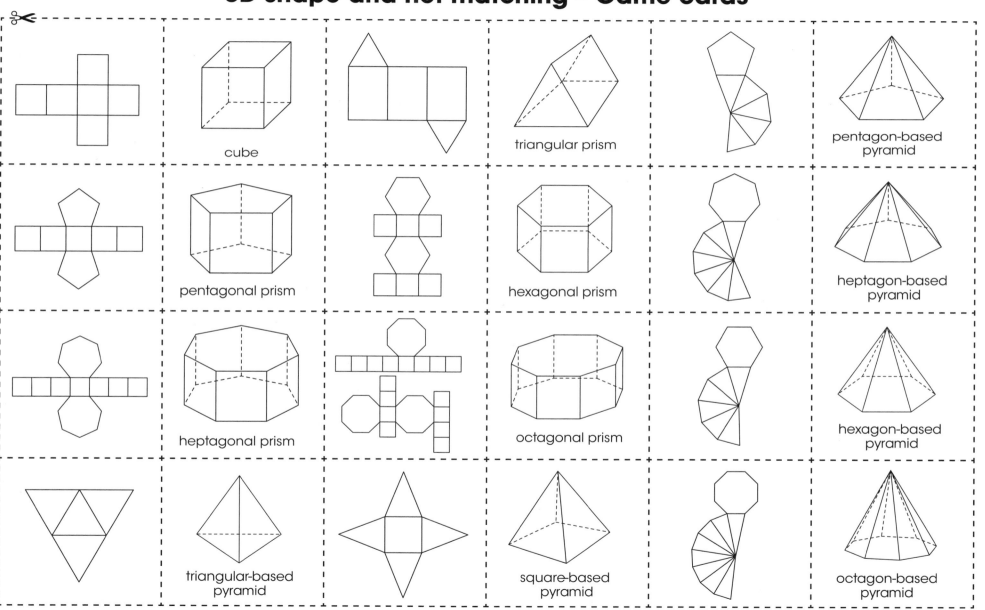

cube

triangular prism

pentagon-based pyramid

pentagonal prism

hexagonal prism

heptagon-based pyramid

heptagonal prism

octagonal prism

hexagon-based pyramid

triangular-based pyramid

square-based pyramid

octagon-based pyramid

The translation game – Game board

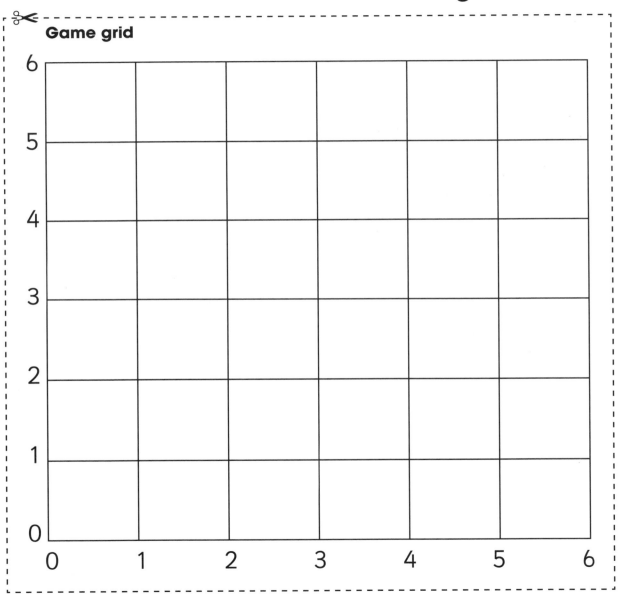

Game grid

Player pieces

Player One starts with the corners of their triangle on (0 ,0), (1, 0) and (0, 2)

Player Two starts with the corners of their triangle on (6, 4), (6, 6) and (5, 6)

Mass bingo

Maths focus: converting larger to smaller metric units of mass.

A game for three to six players

You will need:
- Game cards (page 60).
- Game boards (page 61).
- 12 counters for each player.

How to play

1. One player acts as the bingo caller. The caller shuffles the game cards and places them face down in a pile. The other players take a game board each and a set of counters.
2. The bingo caller turns over each game card in turn and calls out the mass written on the card. The other players look to see if the corresponding mass is on their game board. If it is, they cover it with a counter.
3. The winner is the first player to cover all 12 sections of their game board with counters, and calls out 'Bingo'.

Digital clock matching game

Maths focus: telling and comparing the time using digital clocks with the 12-hour and 24-hour clocks.

A game for two players.

You will need:
- Game cards (page 62).

How to play

1. Shuffle the cards and spread them face down on a table.
2. Players take turns to turn over two cards in position. If the times on the cards match, e.g. 06:09 and 18:09, the player keeps the two cards. If they do not match then the player returns the cards face down.
3. The game ends when all the cards have been taken. The player who has taken the most cards is the winner.

Mass bingo – Game cards

0.1 kg	1 kg	1.9 kg	2.8 kg
0.2 kg	1.1 kg	2 kg	2.9 kg
0.3 kg	1.2 kg	2.1 kg	3 kg
0.4 kg	1.3 kg	2.2 kg	3.1 kg
0.5 kg	1.4 kg	2.3 kg	3.2 kg
0.6 kg	1.5 kg	2.4 kg	3.3 kg
0.7 kg	1.6 kg	2.5 kg	3.4 kg
0.8 kg	1.7 kg	2.6 kg	3.5 kg
0.9 kg	1.8 kg	2.7 kg	3.6 kg

Mass bingo – Game boards

100 g	1100 g	2000 g	2800 g
400 g	1500 g	2300 g	3200 g
700 g	1800 g	2700 g	3600 g

200 g	1000 g	1900 g	2900 g
500 g	1200 g	2000 g	3100 g
700 g	1700 g	2500 g	3500 g

300 g	1200 g	2100 g	3000 g
400 g	1300 g	2300 g	3300 g
900 g	1600 g	2500 g	3400 g

500 g	1100 g	2200 g	2900 g
600 g	1400 g	2400 g	3100 g
800 g	1800 g	2600 g	3300 g

100 g	1000 g	1900 g	2800 g
300 g	1300 g	2100 g	3000 g
600 g	1700 g	2600 g	3500 g

Digital clock matching game – Game cards

Making appointments

Maths focus: comparing 12-hour and 24-hour times and reading timetables using the 24-hour clock.

A game for two players

You will need:
- A game board for each player (page 64).
- Game cards (page 65).

How to play
1. Shuffle the appointment request cards and place them in a pile face down on the table.
2. Players take turns to turn over a card. If they can fit the appointment on the card into their game board at the right time they keep the card and write the name next to the time in the game board. If they cannot fit the appointment into the correct space they pass the card to their opponent who can either keep the card if they can fit in the appointment or place it to the bottom of the pile.
3. The winner is the first player to successfully schedule eight appointments.

Rectangle areas

Maths focus: understanding area measured in square centimetres (cm²).

A game for two players

You will need:
- Game board (page 66).
- A spinner (page 67).
- Pencil and paper clip to make the spinner.
- Two coloured pencils of different colours.

How to play
1. Players use a game board with area 100 cm². They take turns to spin the spinner and colour a rectangle with the area shown on the spinner. The rectangle must not use squares already shaded by either player.
2. Play continues until one player cannot shade a rectangle with the correct area on the grid. The other player is the winner.
3. There is another grid provided for a second game.

Making appointments – Game boards

Today's appointments

Time	Name
10:00	
10:20	
10:40	
11:00	
11:20	
11:40	
12:00	
12:20	
12:40	
13:00	
13:20	
13:40	
14:00	
14:20	
14:40	
15:00	

Today's appointments

Time	Name
10:00	
10:20	
10:40	
11:00	
11:20	
11:40	
12:00	
12:20	
12:40	
13:00	
13:20	
13:40	
14:00	
14:20	
14:40	
15:00	

Making appointments – Game cards

"My name is **Clara**. Can I have an appointment between 2 and 3 this afternoon?"	"This is **Jon**. I need an appointment before midday."	"Please make an appointment for **Tom** between 10 and 11."	"I'd like an appointment after 1 o'clock. This is **Mica**."
"I'd like an appointment between 12 and 1. My name's **Ali**."	"This is **Sally**. Can I have an appointment after half past 2?"	"My name is **Sam**. Can I have an appointment between half 11 and 12?"	"This is **Amy**. I need an appointment after midday."
"Please make an appointment for **Ria** before half past 10."	"I'd like an appointment after 2 o'clock. This is **Emma**."	"I'd like an appointment before 11. My name's **Emma**."	"This is **Sandra**. Can I have an appointment after half past 1?"
"My name is **Dan**. Can I have an appointment at 2 pm?"	"This is **James**. I need an appointment at 11 am."	"Please make an appointment for **Hari** at 1 pm."	"I'd like an appointment at 3 o'clock. This is **Clare**."
"Please give me an appointment at midday. I'm **Tod**."	"This is **Lila**. I'd like an appointment before half past 10 please."	"This is **Bea**. Please give me an appointment between 11 and 12."	"I'm **Ben**. I'd like an appointment between 1 and 2 o'clock."
"I'd like an appointment at 10am please. This is **Zac**."	"My name is **Cal**. I need an appointment before 1 pm."	"Please make an appointment for **Kyle** after a quarter to 2."	"Please make an appointment for **Grace** before a quarter past 11."

Rectangle – Games board

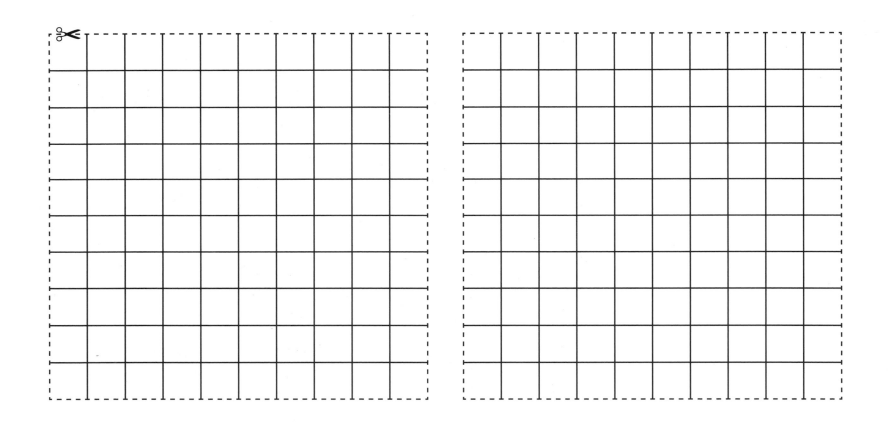

Rectangle areas – spinner template

What to do:

1. Cut out the spinner.
2. Lay a paper clip flat on top of the spinner, so that one end of it lies at the centre of the spinner.
3. Push the point of a pencil through the hole in the end of the paper clip and through the centre of the spinner.
4. Hold the pencil firmly and spin the paper clip around to generate areas.

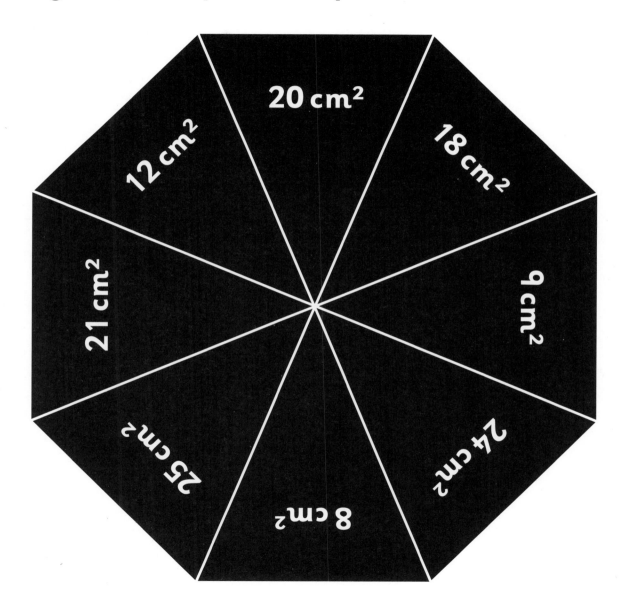

Perimeter bubbles

Maths focus: calculating the perimeter of regular polygons.

A game for two to six players.

You will need:
- A spinner (page 69).
- Pencil and paper clip to make the spinner.
- Game cards (page 69).
- A pile of small sticks, e.g. craft matchsticks.
- Paper for jottings.

How to play
1. Each player starts with three matchsticks which they form into an equilateral triangle. The game cards are shuffled. Then each player takes one card and the other cards are discarded for the rest of the game.
2. The players must imagine that each stick they have is the length shown on the card. So they have an equilateral triangle that has three sides the length of the measurement on their card. Each player should work out and write down their starting perimeter.
3. The players take turns to spin the spinner. They take more sticks according to the number shown on the spinner and add them to their shape to make a larger regular polygon with more sides. Again, they imagine that all the sticks are the length written on their card. They work out and write down the new perimeter.

4. The growing regular polygon is the players 'bubble'. If the perimeter reaches over 60 cm the 'bubble' bursts and the player is out of the game. It is up to each player to decide when to stop spinning the spinner and fix their bubble's perimeter for the game. Play continues until all players fix their bubbles.
5. The winner is the player with an unburst bubble with a perimeter closest to 60 cm.

Measuring lines

Maths focus: measuring lines to nearest millimetre.

A game for two or more players

You will need:
- Game cards (page 70).
- Plain paper; sharp pencils; rulers.
- A straight unmarked edge for each player.

How to play
1. Shuffle the cards and place them face down in a pile.
2. Turn over one card. All players use their unmarked straight edge and sharp pencil to draw a line that they estimate is close to the measurement on the card.
3. The players pass the line they have drawn clockwise around the group. They measure the line that they receive to the nearest millimetre. The player who drew the line can check that the other player is measuring accurately. They work out the difference between the line measured and the length on the card in millimetres.
4. The player with the least difference between the line they drew and the length on the card scores a point.
5. After 10 cards have been played, the player with the most points is the winner.

Perimeter bubbles – spinner template

What to do:
1. Cut out the spinner.
2. Lay a paper clip flat on top of the spinner, so that one end of it lies at the centre of the spinner.
3. Push the point of a pencil through the hole in the end of the paper clip and through the centre of the spinner.
4. Hold the pencil firmly and spin the paper clip around to generate numbers.

Perimeter bubbles – Game cards

3 cm	4 cm	5 cm	6 cm
7 cm	8 cm	9 cm	3 cm
4 cm	5 cm	6 cm	7 cm
8 cm	9 cm	7 cm	8 cm

Measuring lines – Game cards

12.5 cm	21.7 cm	8.1 cm	9.4 cm
14.8 cm	19.2 cm	10.9 cm	5.3 cm
17.6 cm	13.7 cm	202 cm	144 cm
103 cm	86 cm	195 cm	130 cm
221 cm	159 cm	64 cm	118 cm

Modelling against the clock

Maths focus: measuring time in minutes and seconds and adding amounts of time together.

A game for two teams of up to six players and umpires

You will need:
- Game cards (page 72).
- Modelling clay.
- Stopwatches for the umpires.

How to play

1. The game cards are shuffled and placed face down on the table.
2. One player from the first team takes a card and does not show it to anybody else.
3. The umpires with stopwatches press the start button and the player begins to make a model of the object written on the card using the modelling clay.
4. The player's team tries to guess which object is being modelled. Once they guess correctly, the stopwatches are stopped and the time for that team is recorded.
5. The second team takes a turn.
6. Play continues until all players have made a model.
7. The times for each team are added up by the teams. The faster team (which means it has the shorter time) wins the game.

Four-in-a-row calendar game

Maths focus: using a calendar to calculate time intervals in days and weeks.

A game for two players

You will need:
- Game board (page 73).
- A dice.
- Counters in two colours, one colour for each player.

How to play

1. Player 1 rolls the dice. They can place a counter on any date on the calendar that is dice score more or less than a multiple of seven by the value of the dice score.

Example: If a player throws a 3, then they can place a counter on any number that is three more than a multiple of 7, such as '24' or any number that is three less than a multiple of seven, such as '18'.

2. Player 2 throws the dice and places a counter on any date in the way described in point 1.
3. Only one counter can be on a given date. If all possible dates are already taken so that a player is unable to place a counter, play passes to the other player.
4. Play continues until a player makes an unbroken line of four of their counters – horizontally, vertically or diagonally. That player is the winner. If neither player is able to make a line of four then the game is a draw.

Modelling against the clock – Game cards

cat	apple	cube	teddy bear	car
cup	ball	shoe	plate	spoon
candle	eight	pyramid	ruler	snail

October	M	T	W	T	F	S	S
		1	2	3	4	5	6
	7	8	9	10	11	12	13
	14	15	16	17	18	19	20
	21	22	23	24	25	26	27
	28	29	30	31			

Four-in-a-row calendar game – Game board

The largest area game

Maths focus: using the formula for the area of a rectangle to calculate the rectangle's area.

A game for two players

You will need:
- A 1–6 dice (CD-ROM).
- Two sheets of plain or centimetre squared paper.
- A sharp pencil for each player.
- A centimetre ruler for each player.

How to play

1. Each player draws a right-angled corner made with two 1 cm line at the bottom left corner of their sheet of paper. If more support is needed, use centimetre-squared paper.
2. Players take turns to roll the dice. They use their pencil and ruler to continue one of their lines by the number of centimetres shown on the dice.
3. Players take it in turns to roll the dice until they have both rolled four times, each time choosing which line to extend.
4. Once both players have completed their four turns they have drawn two adjacent sides of a rectangle. They draw two more lines to complete the rectangle.
5. The players measure the length and width of their rectangle to the nearest centimetre and calculate the area.
6. The player with the rectangle that has the largest area is the winner.

   Example starting corner:

The quadrilateral perimeter game

Maths focus: measuring the perimeter of irregular polygons.

A game for up to nine players

You will need:
- A set of dominoes (CD-ROM).
- Rulers and sharp pencils.

How to play

1. Shuffle the dominoes and place them face down in a pile.
2. Each player takes three dominoes. Players decide which way round to put each domino to make three two-digit numbers with one decimal place.

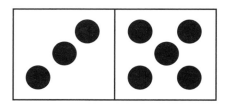

Example: The domino with numbers 3 and 5 could be 3.5 or 5.3.

3. The three dominoes provide the player with the lengths in centimetres of three sides of a quadrilateral.
4. The player constructs a quadrilateral using the three lengths from the dominoes, completing the shape by joining the remaining two corners together.
5. The player measures the last side of the quadrilateral and adds it to the total of the three other sides to find the perimeter.
6. The player whose quadrilateral has a perimeter closest to 20 cm is the winner.

Fill the jug

Maths focus: converting between millilitres and litres.

A game for two players

You will need:
- Game cards (page 76) or blank paper.
- A spinner (page 77).
- Pencil and paper clip to make the spinner.

How to play

1. Players take a game card or draw a jug on a piece of paper.
2. All players start with 0 ml in their jug.
3. The first player spins the spinner. They add the amount pointed to by the spinner to the contents of their jug by drawing a line across the jug and writing the amount next to the line.
4. Players take turns to spin the spinner and add the amount to their jug, keeping a running total of the amount.
5. Players can choose to stop spinning the spinner, and adding to their jug, at any turn. Once they have stopped they must not spin again.
6. If the amount in a player's jug becomes greater than 3000 ml (3 litres) the jug overflows, and they are out of the game.
7. Once all players have stopped spinning the spinner, the player with the jug that has the closest amount to 3000 ml (3 litres), and has not overflowed, is the winner.

It is always beneficial for children to use real equipment and water. If available, use jugs that will hold 3 litres of water and a measuring jug (up to 1.5 litres) to measure the amounts to pour into their jug after each spin.

Example:

1100 ml
500 ml

Time matching

Maths focus: telling and comparing the time using digital and analogue clocks using the 24-hour clock.

A game for two or more players

You will need:
- For each player, 16 sticks of the same size (e.g. craft matchsticks, lolly sticks, pencils).
- Two cubes for each player, to act as the ':' sign.
- Game cards (page 78).
- An 'am' / 'pm' spinner (page 79).

How to play

1. Shuffle the game cards and place them face down in a pile on the table.
2. Each player arranges their sticks and cubes into the 24-hour clock time '01:01'.
3. The top game card is turned over, the 'am / pm' spinner is used to select whether the time shown is before or after noon, and the stopwatch / timer is started.
4. Players do not have enough matchsticks to make every time exactly. They have one minute to rearrange their sticks to make a 24-hour clock time as close as possible to the time shown on the game card.
   After one minute all players must agree what time is shown on the game card and each player calculates the difference between the digital time they have made and the time on the game card.
5. The player(s) whose time is closest to that on the card wins the round.
6. Continue playing by turning over another card and spinning the spinner. Players should decide how many rounds they will have.

Fill the jug – Game cards

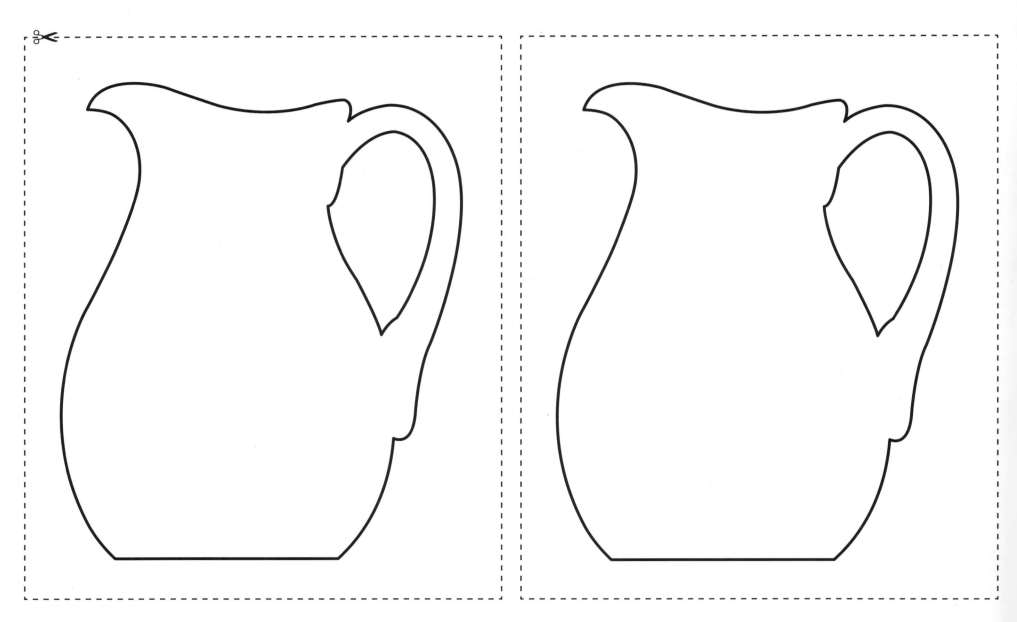

Fill the jug – spinner template

What to do:

1. Cut out the spinner.
2. Lay a paper clip flat on top of the spinner, so that one end of it lies at the centre of the spinner.
3. Push the point of a pencil through the hole in the end of the paper clip and through the centre of the spinner.
4. Hold the pencil firmly and spin the paper clip around to generate volumes.

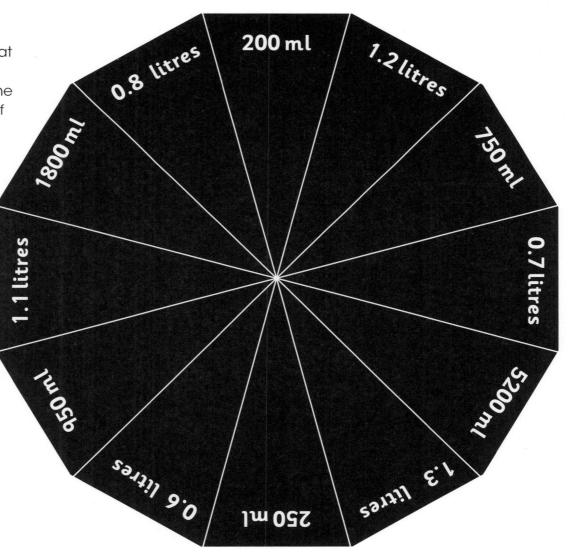

Time matching – Game cards

Time matching – 'am' / 'pm' spinner template

What to do:

1. Cut out the spinner.
2. Lay a paper clip flat on top of the spinner, so that one end of it lies at the centre of the spinner.
3. Push the point of a pencil through the hole in the end of the paper clip and through the centre of the spinner.
4. Hold the pencil firmly and spin the paper clip around to generate am or pm.

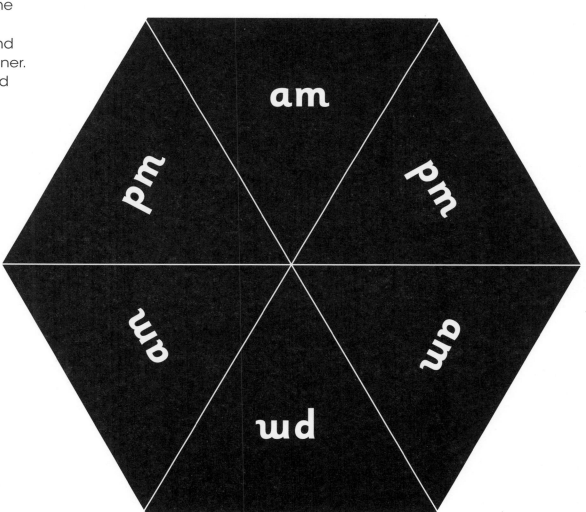

The area game

Maths focus: using the formula for the area of a rectangle to calculate the rectangle's area.

A game for two players

You will need:
- Game cards (page 81).
- 36 counters.
- Game board (page 82).

How to play

1. Shuffle the game cards and place them in a pile face down on the table.
2. Player 1 turns over an game card. They work out the possible lengths and widths of a rectangle that would give that area.
3. Player 1 now looks at the game board to find squares with measurements that match one of the possible length and width pairs. The player places a counter on each square of the pair.

Example: If a player turns over the '36 cm' card, they could cover two '6 cm' squares, or they could cover a '4 cm' square and a '19 cm' square.

4. Player 2 should check that the two squares covered multiply together to make the correct area.
5. Players take turns to take a card and cover a pair of measurements on the grid, with the other player checking this is done correctly.
6. Players cannot place counters on a measurement that already has a counter on it.
7. When one player cannot place their counters on a pair of measurements to match the area on the card, the other player is declared the winner.

The area game – Game cards

4 cm²	8 cm²	10 cm²	12 cm²
15 cm²	18 cm²	20 cm²	21 cm²
25 cm²	28 cm²	30 cm²	32 cm²
35 cm²	36 cm²	40 cm²	45 cm²
54 cm²	56 cm²	60 cm²	100 cm²

2 cm	7 cm	8 cm	5 cm	3 cm	4 cm
9 cm	8 cm	6 cm	2 cm	4 cm	7 cm
3 cm	10 cm	6 cm	9 cm	5 cm	2 cm
7 cm	5 cm	8 cm	4 cm	6 cm	10 cm
9 cm	7 cm	2 cm	3 cm	10 cm	8 cm
6 cm	9 cm	10 cm	5 cm	7 cm	4 cm

Shape values

Maths focus: collecting and analysing data to solve a problem by recording information in a organised way.

A game for two to four players

You will need:
- Game board (page 84).
- Game cards (page 85).
- A working sheet for each player (optional, see page 86).
- A 1–6 dice (CD-ROM).
- A counter for each player.

How to play
1. Shuffle the game cards and place them in a pile face down.
2. Each player places their counter on the start, marked on the game board.
3. Players take turns to roll the dice and move their counter round the board.
4. Any player who lands on CHANCE takes a game card, uses the information and returns the card to the bottom of the pile.
5. The first player to find the values for all six shapes to the satisfaction of the other players is the winner.

Answers:

$\triangle = 2$, $\blacksquare = 5$, $\bullet = 7$, $\langle\rangle = 1$, $\blacksquare = 4$, $\bullet = 2$

During the game player have access to clue cards when they land on CHANCE on the board. Using the 'working out' sheets will encourage players to record the information they are given in an organised way, helping them to analyse their data and draw conclusions from them. There is also an aspect of number problem-solving to this game.

Can you escape from the maze?

Maths focus: understanding the concept of likelihood.

A game for one player

You will need:
- Game board (page 87).
- A coin.

How to play
1. Start at the entrance to the maze.
2. Toss the coin. Follow H ➤ if the coin falls on heads and T ➤ if it falls on tails.
3. Continue until you reach the watch and the exit or until you get stuck with the White Rabbit.

Do you think it is certain, likely, unlikely or impossible to reach the watch?

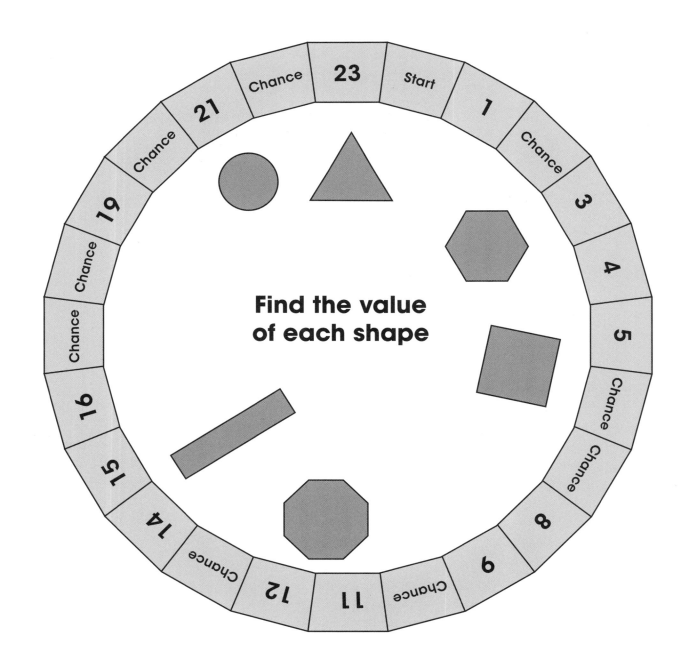

Find the value
of each shape

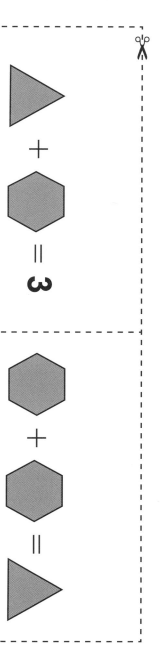

Shape values – working sheet

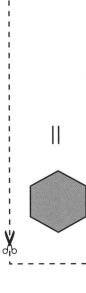
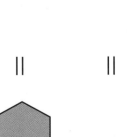
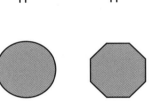

=

=

=

=

=

=

Use this space for working:

=

=

=

=

=

=

Use this space for working:

Entrance

Exit

Handling data trail

Maths focus: interpreting graphs, charts and tables.

A game for two or more players

You will need:
- Game cards (pages 89–106).
- A trail recording sheet for each player or pair of players (CD-ROM).

Preparation
- Photocopy the game cards and place them in a prominent position around the room (numbers in order). Photocopy and distribute a recording sheet to each player or pair of players.

How to play
1. Players can start at any card.
2. They record the number at the top of the card in their loop, answer the question and record the answer in the next position on the loop.
3. They make their way to the card showing that number and continue until the loop is complete.
4. An alternative to a classroom trail is to reduce the cards in size and give a set to a pairs of players to place in a loop.

Answers (start anywhere in the sequence):
26 → 39 → 6 → 30 → 14 → 36 → 13 → 23 → 8 → 35 → 45 → 25 → 50 → 40 → 65 → 4 → 55 → 3 → **26**

Find a pair (mode)

Maths focus: finding the mode of a set of data.

A game for two players

You will need:
- Game cards (page 107).

How to play
1. Shuffle the cards and spread them face down on the table.
2. Players take turns to choose two cards. If the cards match, the player keeps them. If the cards do not match they are replaced in their original position on the table.
3. When all the cards have been chosen the players count their cards.
4. The winner is the player with the most cards.

Example: These are matching cards.

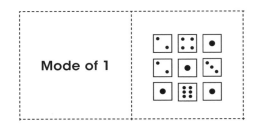

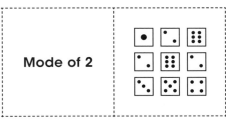

3

The bar line graph shows the frequency of rolling each number.
How many times was an odd number rolled?

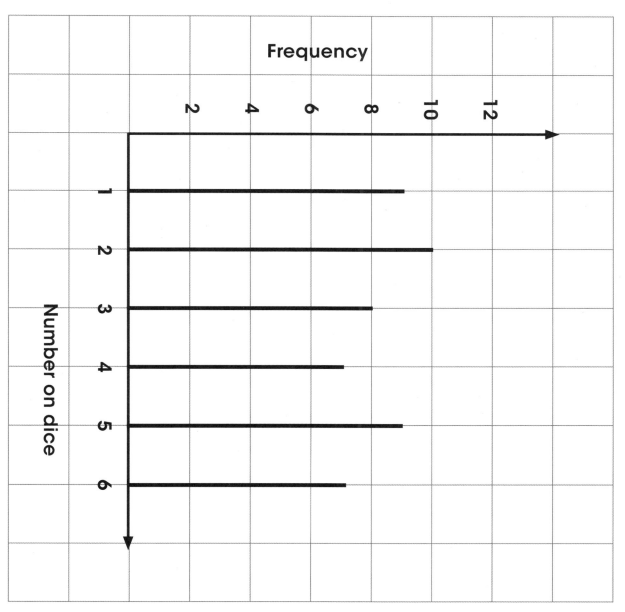

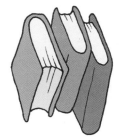

26

When Sara has a fever her temperature rises above normal.
What is her highest temperature in °C?

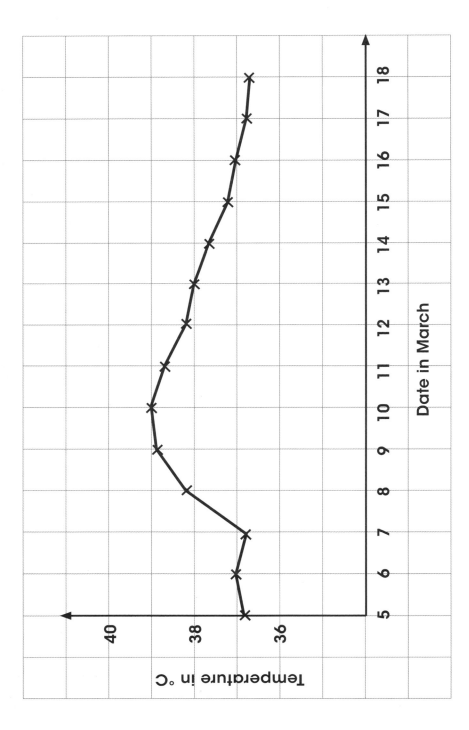

Temperature in °C

40

38

36

Date in March

5   6   7   8   9   10   11   12   13   14   15   16   17   18

39

The chart shows the weather around the world during one day. What was the difference in the maximum temperatures, in °C, between Beijing and New York?

Town or city	Maximum temperature (°C)
Athens (Greece)	17
Beijing (China)	14
Berlin (Germany)	15
Cairo (Egypt)	20
Helsinki (Finland)	15
Istanbul (Turkey)	17
New York (USA)	8

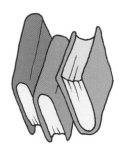

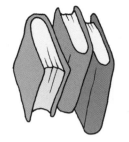

Wayne measures the depth of water in the garden pond each week.
He plots his results on a graph.
What was the depth of water, in centimetres, on 16 July?

Depth of water (in cms)

50
40
30
20
10

2 July   9 July   16 July   23 July   30 July

Date

30

The bar chart shows the number of goals the school football team scored in the league last season.
How many matches did they play?

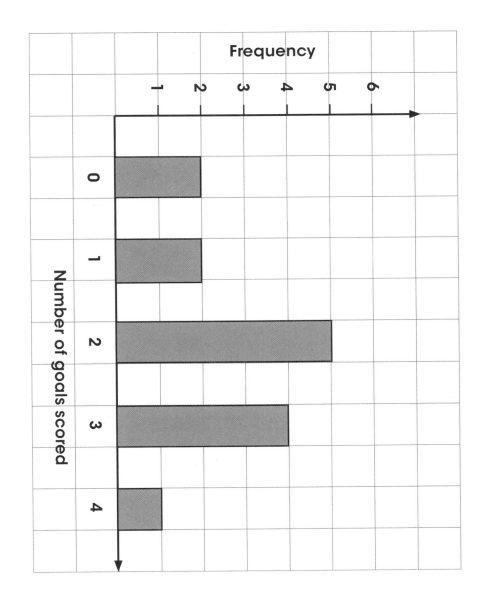

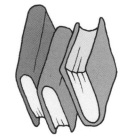

14

Myrtle counts the number of letters in 50 words. She records her results in a tally chart.
How many words have 2, 3 or 4 letters?

Number of letters	Tally
1				
2	‖‖‖‖ ‖‖‖
3	‖‖‖‖ ‖‖‖‖
4	‖‖‖‖	
5			
6		
7			
8		
9		
10	

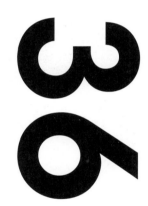

36

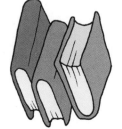

Gabriela kept a record of the classroom temperature.
What was the temperature in °C at 3:00 pm?

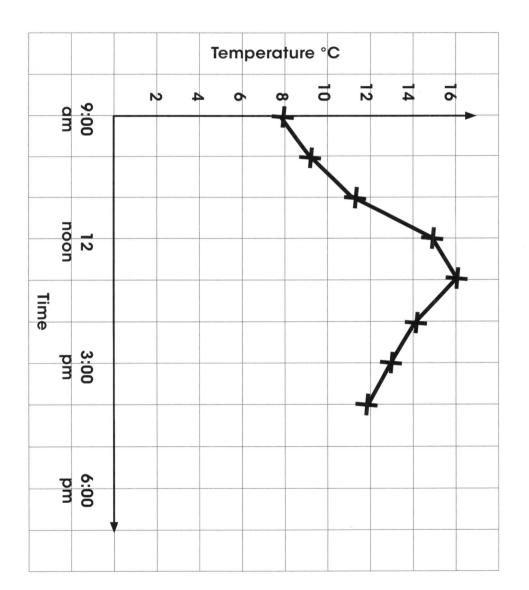

Temperature °C

16
14
12
10
8
6
4
2

9:00 am   12 noon   3:00 pm   6:00 pm

Time

13

Here are the sunrise and sunset times for four days in July.
How many minutes later is the sunrise on 27 July than on 6 July?

Date	Sunrise	Sunset
6 July	04:54	21:18
13 July	05:00	21:12
20 July	05:09	21:05
27 July	05:17	20:55

23

The graph shows the number of children in the families of Year 5 students.
How many families have more than two children?

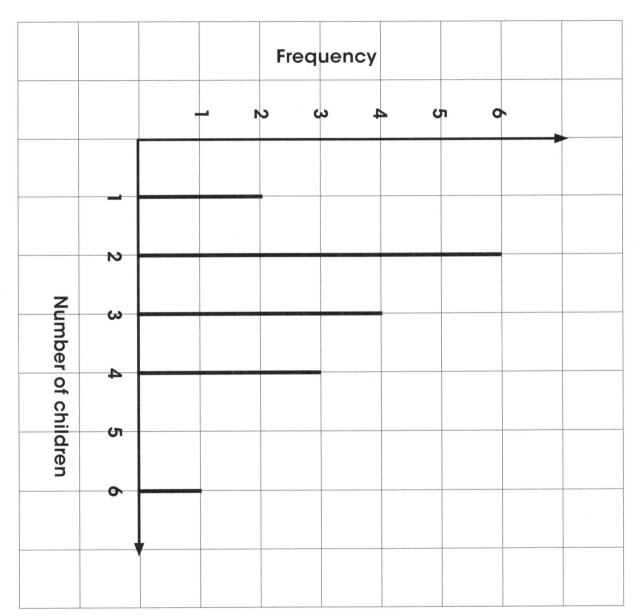

Frequency

Number of children

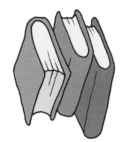

In a survey, the students in Grange School are asked to choose their favourite fruit drink.

The graph shows the results of the survey.

How many more students chose orange than pineapple?

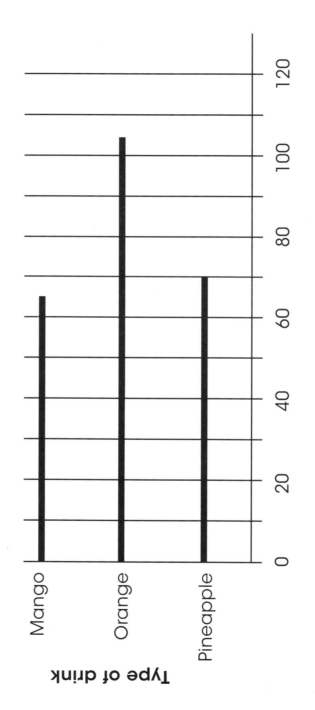

Type of drink

Mango

Orange

Pineapple

Number of students

0   20   40   60   80   100   120

The graph shows how far five children can swim.
How many metres can Cindy swim?

35

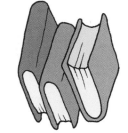

Children

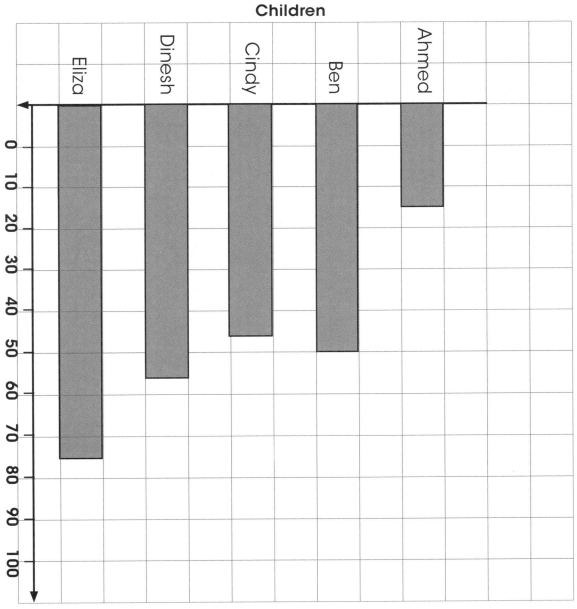

Eliza

Dinesh

Cindy

Ben

Ahmed

0 10 20 30 40 50 60 70 80 90 100

Distance in metres

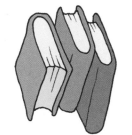

45

The pictogram shows how many bikes Hamad sells in a bike shop.
How many bikes does he sell altogether?

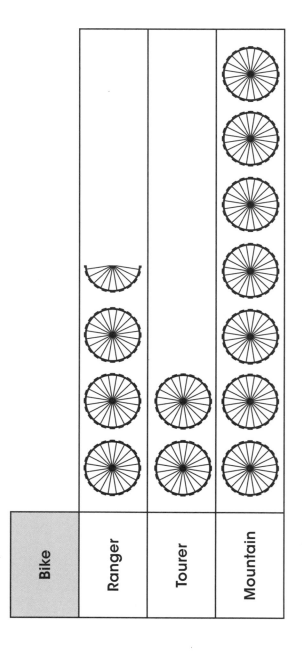

Bike				
Ranger				
Tourer				
Mountain				

 represents 2 bikes

25

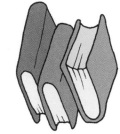

The graph shows how the temperature of a pot of liquid decreases as it cools.
Ahmed takes a reading after 10 minutes.
What is the temperature in °C?

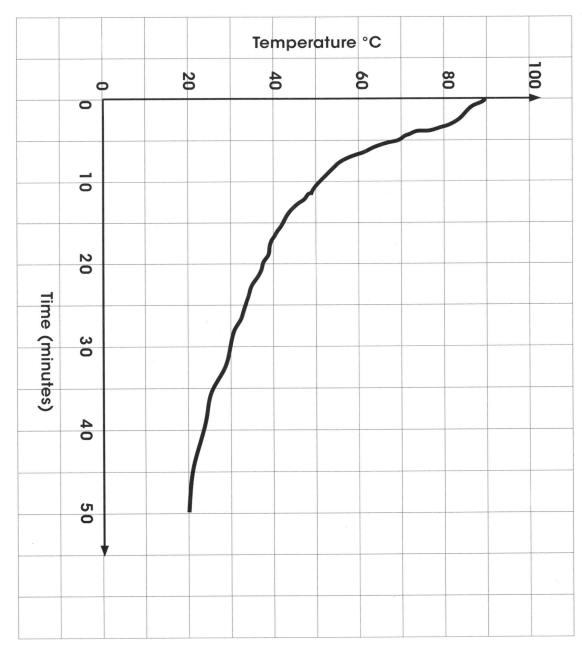

Temperature °C

Time (minutes)

50

The students in class 5 visit a forest one day each week for six weeks.
Each week they collect acorns and pine cones.
How many acorns do they collect in week 4?

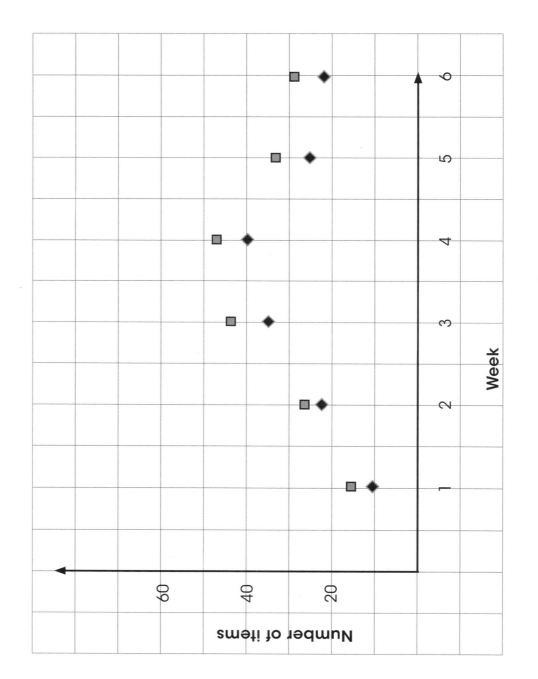

◆ acorn

■ pine cone

A group of students took part in an activity session.
Each student chose one activity.
How many students chose running or cycling?

40

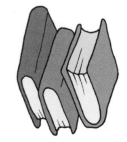

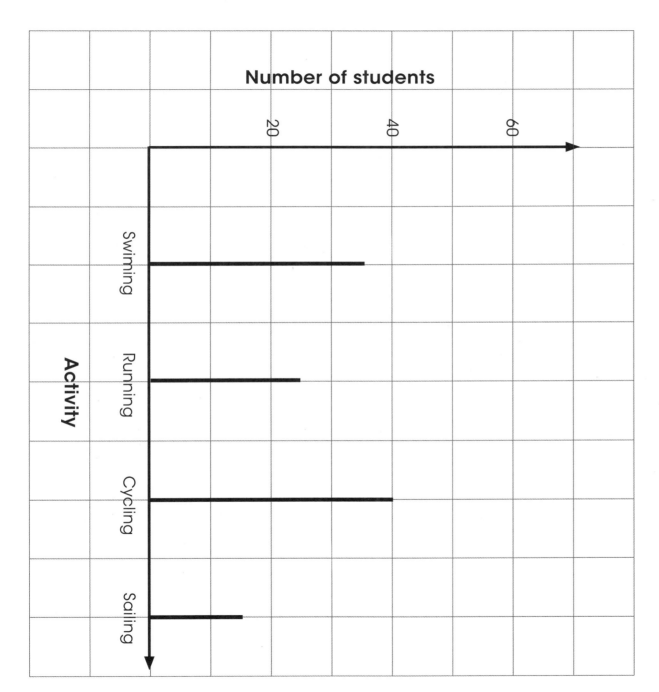

Number of students

20

40

60

Activity

Swiming

Running

Cycling

Sailing

65

Five students ran in two races on sports day. The table shows their times.
In the 800 m race, how many seconds did Conrad finish ahead of Leroy?

	100 m race	800 m race
Abdul	15.8 seconds	3 minutes 02 seconds
Dinesh	19.8 seconds	2 minutes 58 seconds
Leroy	16.7 seconds	3 minutes 01 seconds
Cheng	17.1 seconds	2 minutes 59 seconds
Conrad	18.4 seconds	2 minutes 57 seconds

The graph shows the number of cars in a car park at different times during one day.
There are 100 cars in the car park when it is full.
How many empty spaces were there in the car park at 1 pm?

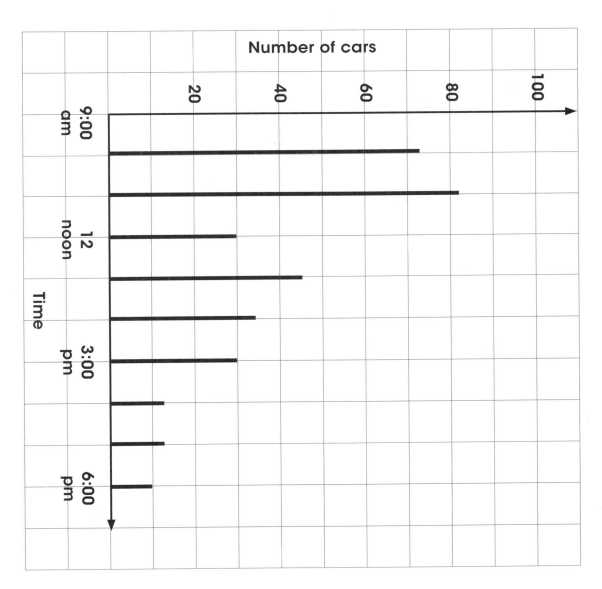

Number of cars

100

80

60

40

20

9:00 am

12 noon

Time

3:00 pm

6:00 pm

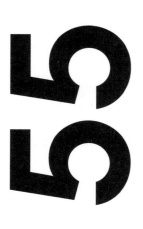

55

The table shows when flights take off at an airport.
How many flights take off between 12 noon and 2pm?

Flight number	Destination	Take-off time
EZ208	Tel Aviv	09:00
OB123	Bucharest	10:00
EZ215	Amsterdam	11:00
FR351	Lanzarote	11:30
EZ904	Berlin	11:55
EZ212	Nice	12:05
EZ245	Zurich	12:50
FR842	Kerry	13:45
WB622	Budapest	14:25

Find a pair (mode) – Game cards

Mode of 1	Mode of 2	Mode of 4	Mode of 5	Mode of 6

Mode of 2	Mode of 3	Mode of 4	Mode of 5	Mode of 6